OSTEOPORO
PREVENTION COOKBOOK

Promote Your Bone Health with Over 150 Delicious and Calcium-Rich Recipes to Strengthen Bones and Enhance Vitality

Arielle Curbert

Dear valued customers,

We want to take a moment to express our heartfelt appreciation for your unwavering support and loyalty. Your trust in our products and services means the world to us, and we are deeply grateful for the opportunity to serve you.

Every day, we strive to exceed your expectations and provide you with exceptional experiences that bring joy and satisfaction. Your feedback, encouragement, and enthusiasm drive us to continually improve and innovate, ensuring that we always deliver the best possible results.

Without you, our journey would not be possible. Your support fuels our passion and inspires us to reach new heights. We are honored to be a part of your lives and are committed to earning your trust and loyalty each and every day.

Thank you for choosing us, for believing in us, and for being a cherished member of our community. We look forward to continuing this incredible journey together and to many more moments of shared success and happiness.

With deepest gratitude,

[ARIELLE CURBERT]

Copyright and Disclaimer

Copyright © [2024]

All rights reserved. No part of this book may be reproduced or transmitted in any form or by any means, electronic or mechanical, including photocopying, recording, or by any information storage and retrieval system, without permission in writing from the publisher, except in the case of brief quotations embodied in critical articles and reviews.

The recipes, nutritional information, and other content contained in this book are intended for informational purposes only and are not intended to be used as medical advice, diagnosis, or treatment. The information provided in this book is based on research and expert opinion, but individual needs and circumstances may vary. It is recommended that readers consult with a qualified healthcare professional before making any dietary or lifestyle changes, especially if they have a medical condition or are taking medication.

The author and publisher of this book make no representations or warranties with respect to the accuracy, applicability, fitness, or completeness of the contents of this book. They disclaim any liability for any errors or omissions in the content or for any damages or losses arising from the use of the information provided herein.

INTRODUCTION 8
- A. EXPLANATION OF OSTEOPOROSIS 8
- B. IMPORTANCE OF PREVENTING OSTEOPOROSIS 8
- C. ROLE OF NUTRITION IN BONE HEALTH 9
- D. OVERVIEW OF THE COOKBOOK'S PURPOSE AND STRUCTURE 10

CHAPTER 1: BUILDING BLOCKS FOR STRONG BONES 12
- A. IMPORTANCE OF CALCIUM AND VITAMIN D 12
- B. LIST OF CALCIUM-RICH FOODS 13
- C. RECIPES FEATURING CALCIUM-RICH INGREDIENTS 14

CHAPTER 2: POWER OF PROTEIN 22
- A. PROTEIN'S ROLE IN BONE HEALTH 22
- B. PROTEIN SOURCES FOR STRONG BONES 23
- C. RECIPES INCORPORATING PROTEIN-RICH FOODS 24

CHAPTER 3: ESSENTIAL NUTRIENTS FOR BONE HEALTH 32
- A. OVERVIEW OF OTHER IMPORTANT NUTRIENTS 32
- B. LIST OF FOODS RICH IN MAGNESIUM, PHOSPHORUS, AND VITAMIN K 33
- C. RECIPES FEATURING THESE ESSENTIAL NUTRIENTS 34

CHAPTER 4: FORTIFYING WITH FRUITS AND VEGETABLES 41
- A. ANTIOXIDANTS AND PHYTONUTRIENTS FOR BONE HEALTH 41
- B. FRUITS AND VEGETABLES TO INCLUDE IN THE DIET 42
- C. RECIPES HIGHLIGHTING COLORFUL PRODUCE 43

CHAPTER 5: HEALTHY FATS FOR STRONG BONES 47
- A. IMPORTANCE OF OMEGA-3 FATTY ACIDS 47
- B. SOURCES OF HEALTHY FATS 48
- C. RECIPES FEATURING OMEGA-3-RICH INGREDIENTS 49

CHAPTER 6: BONE-BUILDING BEVERAGES 54
- A. BENEFITS OF BONE-BOOSTING DRINKS 54
- B. RECIPES FOR NUTRIENT-RICH BEVERAGES 55

CHAPTER 7: MEAL PLANNING FOR BONE HEALTH 60
- A. TIPS FOR CREATING BALANCED MEALS 60

    B. Sample meal plans 61
    C. Suggestions for breakfast, lunch, dinner, and snacks 63
        Breakfast 63
        Lunch: 66
        Dinner: 70
        Snacks: 73

CHAPTER 8: BEYOND THE PLATE: LIFESTYLE TIPS FOR STRONG BONES 76

    A. Additional lifestyle factors for bone health 76
    B. Practical tips for maintaining strong bones 77
    C. Strategies for incorporating healthy habits into daily life 78
    D. Sample exercises for stronger bone 79

CONCLUSION 81

    A. Recap of key points 81
    B. Encouragement for readers to prioritize bone health 82
    C. Final thoughts and encouragement to explore the recipes in the cookbook 83

BONUS SECTION 1: QUICK AND EASY BONE-BOOSTING SNACKS 84

    A. Introduction to the importance of snacking for bone health 84
    B. Recipes for convenient and nutritious snacks 85

BONUS SECTION 2: BONE-BUILDING SMOOTHIE BOWLS 88

    A. Introduction to the benefits of smoothie bowls for bone health 88
    B. Recipes for vibrant and nutrient-packed smoothie bowl creations .. 88

BONUS SECTION 3: FAMILY-FRIENDLY BONE-BOOSTING RECIPES 91

    A. Introduction to the importance of involving the whole family in bone-healthy eating habits 91
    B. Recipes that appeal to both adults and children alike 91

BONUS SECTION 4: PLANT-BASED POWERHOUSES FOR STRONG BONES 99

    A. Introduction to plant-based eating for bone health 99

B. Recipes showcasing the abundance of bone-boosting plant foods 99

BONUS SECTION 5: BONE-BUILDING BRUNCH IDEAS 104

A. Introduction to the versatility of brunch options that support bone health 104

B. Recipes for hearty and nutritious brunch dishes perfect for weekend gatherings 104

YOGA EXERCISES FOR STRONGER AND HEALTHY BONES 109

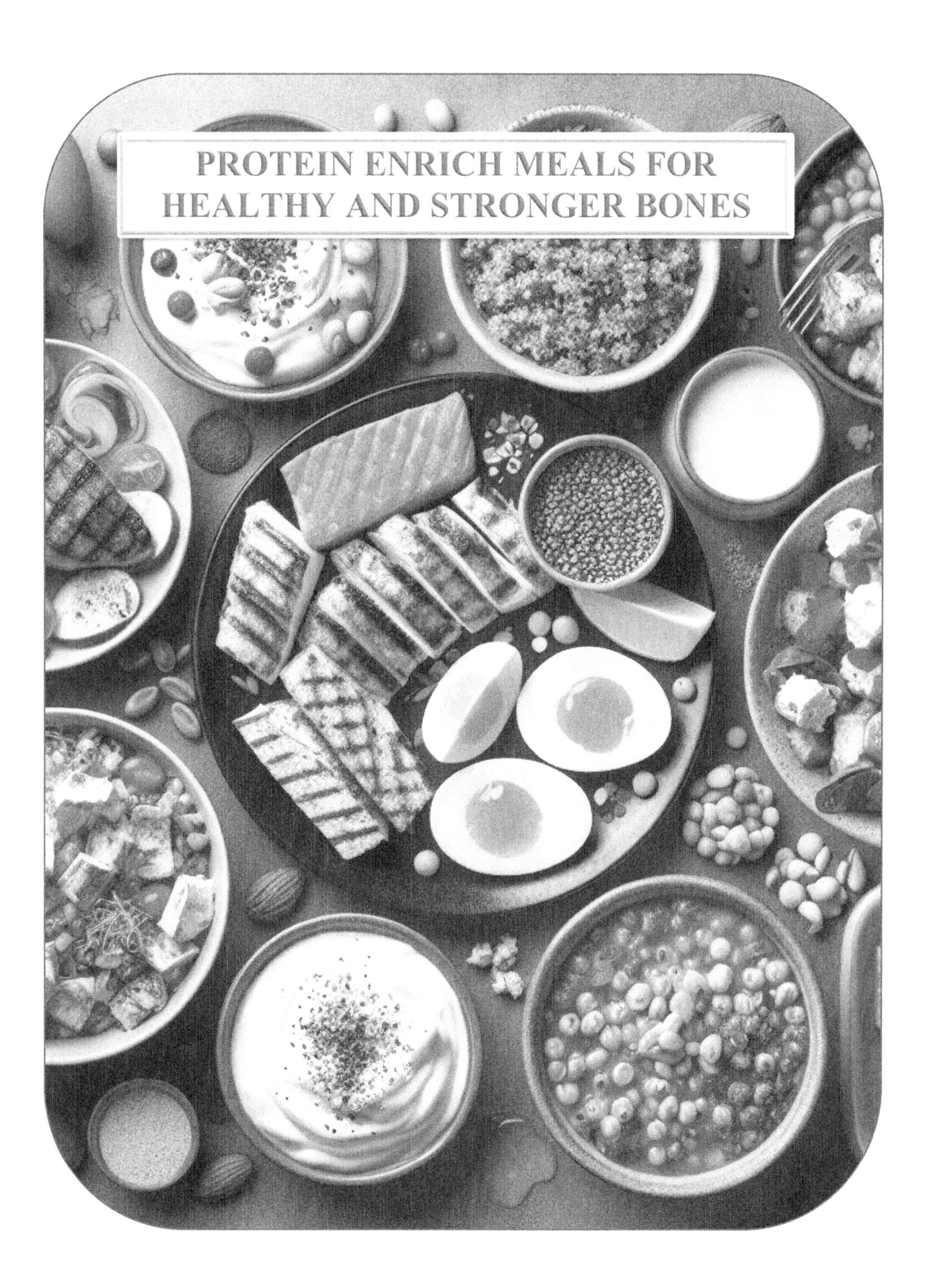

PROTEIN ENRICH MEALS FOR HEALTHY AND STRONGER BONES

Introduction

A. Explanation of osteoporosis

Osteoporosis is a bone disease characterized by weakened bones more susceptible to fractures. It occurs when the density and quality of bone decrease, leading to porous and fragile bones. This condition often develops gradually over the years and may not be noticeable until a fracture occurs. Osteoporosis primarily affects older adults, particularly women after menopause. Still, it can also occur in men and younger individuals due to various factors such as genetics, lifestyle choices, and medical conditions. Understanding osteoporosis is crucial for taking proactive steps to prevent its onset and maintain strong and healthy bones throughout life

B. Importance of preventing osteoporosis

Preventing osteoporosis is essential for maintaining overall health and quality of life, as this condition can significantly impact mobility, independence, and well-being. Here are several reasons why preventing osteoporosis is crucial:

1. Reduced Risk of Fractures: Osteoporosis weakens bones, making them more prone to fractures, especially in the spine, hips, and wrists. By taking steps to prevent osteoporosis, individuals can lower their risk of experiencing debilitating fractures that can lead to pain, disability, and loss of function.
2. Preservation of Bone Health: Preventing osteoporosis involves adopting lifestyle habits and dietary choices that promote optimal bone health. By maintaining strong and dense bones, individuals can reduce the likelihood of developing osteoporosis later in life and enjoy better overall physical resilience.
3. Enhanced Quality of Life: Osteoporosis-related fractures can have a profound impact on daily activities and quality of life. Preventing osteoporosis helps individuals maintain their independence, mobility, and ability to engage in activities they enjoy, leading to a more fulfilling and active lifestyle.
4. Lower Healthcare Costs: Fractures resulting from osteoporosis often require medical treatment, including hospitalization, surgery, and rehabilitation. By preventing osteoporosis, individuals can avoid the financial burden

associated with these healthcare expenses and reduce the strain on healthcare systems.
5. Long-Term Health Benefits: Many of the lifestyle changes and habits that support bone health also contribute to overall well-being and longevity. By prioritizing bone health through preventive measures, individuals can potentially reduce their risk of other chronic conditions such as cardiovascular disease, diabetes, and certain cancers.

C. Role of nutrition in bone health

Nutrition plays a fundamental role in maintaining strong and healthy bones throughout life. Adequate intake of essential nutrients provides the building blocks necessary for bone formation, repair, and maintenance. Here's how nutrition influences bone health:

1. Calcium: Calcium is a key mineral that is essential for building and maintaining bone density. It provides the structural framework for bones and helps to keep them strong and resilient. Dairy products, leafy greens, tofu, almonds, and fortified foods are high in calcium.
2. Vitamin D: Vitamin D is essential for the absorption of calcium in the body. Without enough vitamin D, the body cannot properly utilize calcium, resulting in weakened bones. Exposure to sunlight and consumption of vitamin D-rich foods such as fatty fish, eggs, and fortified dairy products are important for maintaining adequate vitamin D levels.
3. Protein: Protein is crucial for bone health as it provides the amino acids necessary for bone formation and repair. Including protein-rich foods such as lean meats, poultry, fish, beans, lentils, and dairy products in the diet supports optimal bone health.
4. Magnesium: Magnesium plays a role in bone metabolism and helps to regulate calcium levels in the body. Foods rich in magnesium, such as nuts, seeds, whole grains, leafy greens, and legumes, contribute to overall bone health.
5. Phosphorus: Phosphorus works in conjunction with calcium to maintain bone strength and structure. It is found in abundance in protein-rich foods, dairy products, nuts, seeds, and whole grains.

6. **Vitamin K:** Vitamin K is involved in the synthesis of proteins necessary for bone mineralization. Green leafy vegetables, broccoli, Brussels sprouts, and fermented foods are excellent sources of vitamin K.
7. **Antioxidants:** Antioxidants such as vitamins C and E, and phytonutrients found in fruits and vegetables, help to reduce oxidative stress and inflammation, which can contribute to bone loss.

D. Overview of the cookbook's purpose and structure

The purpose of the "Strong Bones Cookbook: Delicious Recipes for Osteoporosis Prevention" is to empower readers with the knowledge and tools to support their bone health through nutrition. This cookbook is designed to provide a comprehensive collection of flavorful and nutritious recipes that incorporate bone-boosting ingredients, helping readers prevent osteoporosis and maintain strong and healthy bones throughout life.

Structured for ease of use and effectiveness, the cookbook is divided into chapters that focus on different aspects of bone health and nutrition. Each chapter is dedicated to exploring a specific category of bone-boosting foods and includes a variety of recipes that showcase these ingredients in delicious and creative ways. The cookbook begins with an introduction that explains the importance of preventing osteoporosis and highlights the role of nutrition in supporting bone health. This section sets the stage for the rest of the book, emphasizing the significance of dietary choices in maintaining strong and resilient bones.

Following the introduction, the cookbook is organized into chapters that cover various nutritional components essential for bone health. Each chapter provides valuable information on the featured nutrients, along with a selection of mouthwatering recipes that incorporate these ingredients. From calcium-rich dairy products to protein-packed meats and plant-based sources, the recipes are designed to appeal to a wide range of tastes and preferences.

In addition to the core recipe chapters, the cookbook includes bonus sections that offer additional value and inspiration to readers. These bonus sections feature specialized recipes, meal planning tips, lifestyle suggestions, and other resources to enhance the reader's journey toward better bone health.

With its practical guidance and delicious recipes, the "Strong Bones Cookbook" is a valuable resource for anyone seeking to prioritize bone health and prevent osteoporosis. Whether you're a seasoned cook or a beginner in the kitchen, this cookbook provides the tools and inspiration you need to nourish your body and support lifelong bone health

Chapter 1: Building Blocks for Strong Bones

A. Importance of calcium and vitamin D

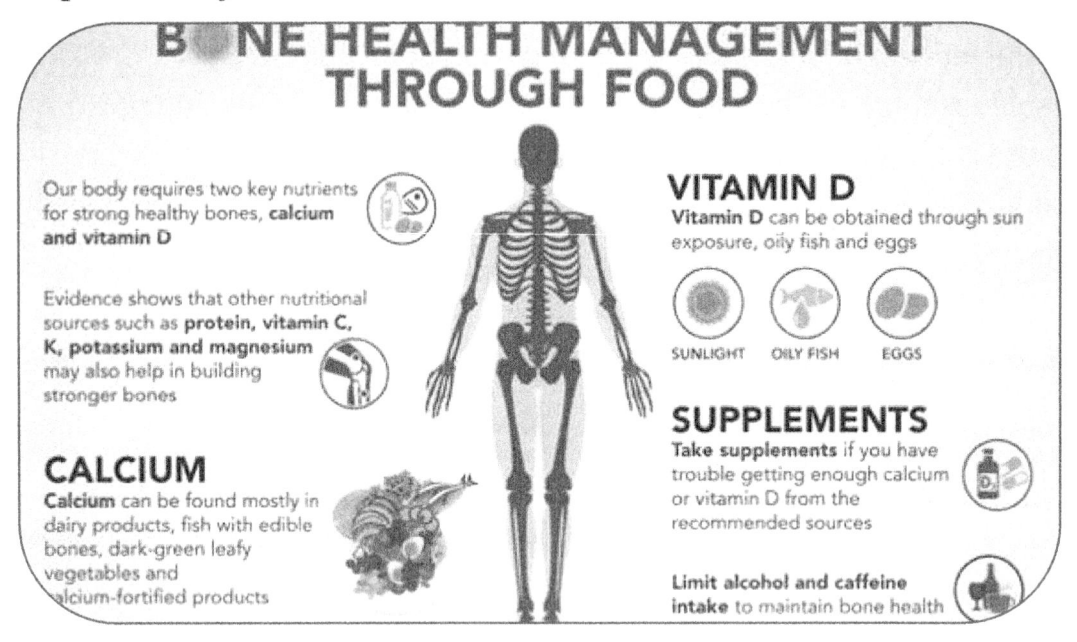

BONE HEALTH MANAGEMENT THROUGH FOOD

Our body requires two key nutrients for strong healthy bones, **calcium and vitamin D**

Evidence shows that other nutritional sources such as **protein, vitamin C, K, potassium and magnesium** may also help in building stronger bones

CALCIUM
Calcium can be found mostly in dairy products, fish with edible bones, dark-green leafy vegetables and calcium-fortified products

VITAMIN D
Vitamin D can be obtained through sun exposure, oily fish and eggs

SUNLIGHT   OILY FISH   EGGS

SUPPLEMENTS
Take **supplements** if you have trouble getting enough calcium or vitamin D from the recommended sources

Limit alcohol and caffeine intake to maintain bone health

Calcium and vitamin D are two essential nutrients that play pivotal roles in maintaining strong and healthy bones. Understanding their importance is crucial for preventing osteoporosis and ensuring optimal bone health. Here's why calcium and vitamin D are so vital:

1. Calcium:
    - Calcium is the primary mineral responsible for building and maintaining bone density and strength. Around 99% of the body's calcium is stored in bones and teeth, where it provides structural support and helps to maintain their integrity.
    - Adequate calcium intake is essential during periods of bone growth and development, such as childhood and adolescence, to ensure proper bone formation and mineralization.
    - Throughout adulthood, calcium continues to play a critical role in maintaining bone density and preventing bone loss, particularly in older adults who may be at higher risk of osteoporosis.
    - In addition to supporting bone health, calcium also contributes to muscle function, nerve transmission, and blood clotting.
    - Sources of calcium include dairy products (such as milk, cheese, and yogurt), fortified plant-based milk alternatives, leafy green vegetables

(such as kale and broccoli), tofu, almonds, and canned fish with bones (such as sardines and salmon).
2. Vitamin D:
   - Vitamin D is required for calcium absorption and utilization in the body. Without sufficient vitamin D, the body cannot effectively absorb calcium from the diet, leading to impaired bone mineralization and increased risk of fractures.
   - Sunlight is the body's primary source of vitamin D production. When exposed to sunlight, the skin produces vitamin D, which is then converted to an active form in the liver and kidneys.
   - However, many people may have limited sun exposure or live in regions where sunlight is scarce, making it challenging to obtain adequate vitamin D from sunlight alone. In such cases, dietary sources and supplements may be necessary to meet vitamin D needs.
   - Food sources of vitamin D include fatty fish (such as salmon, mackerel, and tuna), fortified dairy products, fortified plant-based milk alternatives, egg yolks, and fortified breakfast cereals.
   - Vitamin D also plays a crucial role in immune function, mood regulation, and overall health beyond its role in bone health.

B. List of calcium-rich foods

Including calcium-rich foods in your diet is crucial for maintaining strong and healthy bones. Here is a list of foods that are excellent sources of calcium:
1. Dairy Products:
   - Milk (cow's milk, almond milk, soy milk, etc.)
   - Yogurt (plain or flavored)
   - Cheese (cheddar, mozzarella, Swiss, etc.)
   - Cottage cheese
2. Leafy Greens:
   - Kale
   - Collard greens
   - Spinach
   - Swiss chard
   - Bok choy

3. Fortified Foods:
   - Fortified orange juice
   - Fortified plant-based milk alternatives (almond milk, soy milk, coconut milk, etc.)
   - Fortified breakfast cereals
   - Fortified tofu
4. Fish:
   - Canned fish that contains bones (such as sardines and salmon)
   - Soft-boned canned fish (such as anchovies)
5. Nuts and Seeds:
   - Almonds
   - Sesame seeds
   - Chia seeds
   - Flaxseeds
6. Legumes:
   - Beans (white beans, navy beans, black beans, etc.)
   - Lentils
   - Chickpeas (garbanzo beans)
7. Other Calcium-Rich Foods:
   - Tofu (made with calcium sulfate)
   - Edamame
   - Figs (dried or fresh)
   - Broccoli

C. Recipes featuring calcium-rich ingredients

1. Spinach and Feta Stuffed Chicken Breast

Ingredients:
- 4 boneless, skinless chicken breasts
- 2 cups fresh spinach, chopped
- 1/2 cup crumbled feta cheese
- 1 teaspoon garlic powder
- Salt and pepper to taste
- Olive oil for cooking

Instructions:

1. Preheat the oven to 375°F (190°C).
2. In a mixing bowl, combine the chopped spinach, crumbled feta cheese, garlic powder, salt, and pepper.
3. Make a horizontal slit in each chicken breast to create a pocket.
4. Stuff each chicken breast with the spinach-feta mixture.
5. Heat olive oil in a skillet over medium-high heat. Brown the stuffed chicken breasts for 2-3 minutes on each side.
6. Transfer the browned chicken breasts to a baking dish and bake in the preheated oven for 15-20 minutes or until the chicken is cooked through and no longer pink in the center. Enjoy!

Nutritional Information (per serving): Calories: 280, Protein: 40g, Fat: 10g, Carbohydrates: 3g, Fiber: 1g, Calcium: 150mg Cooking Time: 25 minutes

2. Creamy Broccoli and Cheese Soup

Ingredients:
- 4 cups fresh broccoli florets
- 1 small onion, diced
- 2 cloves garlic, minced
- 4 cups low-sodium chicken or vegetable broth
- 1 cup shredded cheddar cheese
- 1 cup heavy cream or whole milk.
- Salt and pepper to taste
- Olive oil for cooking

Instructions:
1. Heat olive oil in a large pot over medium heat. Add diced onion and minced garlic, and sauté until softened.
2. Add broccoli florets to the pot and pour in the chicken or vegetable broth. Bring to a boil, then reduce heat and simmer for 15-20 minutes, or until broccoli is tender.
3. Using an immersion blender, puree the soup until smooth. Alternatively, carefully transfer the soup to a blender and process until smooth in batches.
4. Return the blended soup to the pot and stir in the shredded cheddar cheese until melted and creamy.
5. Pour in the whole milk or heavy cream, stirring until well combined—season with salt and pepper to taste.

6. Simmer for an additional 5 minutes. Enjoy!

Nutritional Information (per serving): Calories: 220, Protein: 12g, Fat: 15g, Carbohydrates: 10g, Fiber: 3g, Calcium: 250mg Cooking Time: 30 minutes

3. Homemade Yogurt Parfait with Berries and Nuts

Ingredients:
- 2 cups Greek yogurt
- A cup of mixed berries (strawberries, blueberries, raspberries)
- 1/4 cup of chopped nuts (almonds, walnuts, pecans)
- 2 tablespoons of honey or maple syrup (optional)
- 1 teaspoon vanilla extract (optional)

Instructions:
1. In a bowl or glass, layer Greek yogurt with mixed berries and chopped nuts.
2. Drizzle with honey or maple syrup and add a splash of vanilla extract if desired.
3. Repeat the layers until the bowl or glass is filled. Enjoy!

Nutritional Information (per serving): Calories: 250, Protein: 20g, Fat: 10g, Carbohydrates: 20g, Fiber: 3g, Calcium: 300mg Assembly Time: 5 minutes

4. Salmon and Spinach Quiche

Ingredients:
- 1 pre-made pie crust
- 1 cup cooked salmon, flaked
- 2 cups fresh spinach, chopped
- 1/2 cup shredded cheddar cheese
- 4 large eggs
- 1 cup milk
- Salt and pepper to taste

Instructions:
1. Preheat the oven to 375°F (190°C).
2. Place the pre-made pie crust in a pie dish and prick the bottom with a fork.
3. Spread the cooked salmon, chopped spinach, and shredded cheddar cheese evenly over the pie crust.
4. In a mixing bowl, whisk together the eggs, milk, salt, and pepper.
5. Pour the egg mixture over the salmon, spinach, and cheese into the pie crust.

6. Bake in the preheated oven for 35-40 minutes or until the quiche is set and golden brown on top.
7. Allow the quiche to cool slightly before slicing and serving. Enjoy!

Nutritional Information (per serving): Calories: 300, Protein: 20g, Fat: 15g, Carbohydrates: 20g, Fiber: 2g, Calcium: 200mg Cooking Time: 45 minutes

5. Broccoli and Cauliflower Gratin

Ingredients:
- 2 cups broccoli florets
- 2 cups cauliflower florets
- 1/4 cup grated Parmesan cheese
- 1/4 cup shredded mozzarella cheese
- 1/2 cup breadcrumbs
- 1 tablespoon olive oil
- Salt and pepper to taste

Instructions:
1. Preheat the oven to 375°F (190°C).
2. Steam the broccoli and cauliflower florets until tender, then transfer to a baking dish.
3. In a small bowl, combine the Parmesan cheese, mozzarella cheese, breadcrumbs, olive oil, salt, and pepper.
4. Sprinkle the breadcrumb mixture over the steamed broccoli and cauliflower in the baking dish.
5. Bake in the preheated oven for 20-25 minutes or until the gratin is golden and bubbly.
6. Serve hot as a delicious side dish or light main course. Enjoy!

Nutritional Information (per serving): Calories: 180, Protein: 10g, Fat: 8g, Carbohydrates: 15g, Fiber: 4g, Calcium: 150mg Cooking Time: 30 minutes

6. Quinoa and Black Bean Stuffed Bell Peppers

Ingredients:
- 4 large bell peppers, halved and seeded
- 1 cup cooked quinoa
- 1 cup black beans, rinsed and drained
- 1 cup diced tomatoes

- 1/2 cup shredded cheddar cheese
- 1 teaspoon cumin
- 1 teaspoon chili powder
- Salt and pepper to taste

Instructions:
1. Preheat the oven to 375°F (190°C).
2. In a mixing bowl, combine the cooked quinoa, black beans, diced tomatoes, shredded cheddar cheese, cumin, chili powder, salt, and pepper.
3. Stuff each bell pepper half with the quinoa and black bean mixture, pressing down gently to pack the filling.
4. Place the stuffed bell peppers in a baking dish and wrap them in aluminum foil.
5. Bake in the preheated oven for 25-30 minutes or until the peppers are tender and the filling is heated through.
6. Remove the foil and sprinkle additional cheese on top of each stuffed pepper, if desired.
7. Return the peppers to the oven and bake for an additional 5 minutes or until the cheese is melted and bubbly.
8. Serve hot and garnish with chopped fresh cilantro or green onions, if desired. Enjoy!

Nutritional Information (per serving): Calories: 250, Protein: 12g, Fat: 8g, Carbohydrates: 35g, Fiber: 10g, Calcium: 150mg Cooking Time: 40 minutes

7. **Tofu and Vegetable Stir-Fry**

Ingredients:
- 1 firm block of tofu, pressed and cubed
- 2 cups mixed veggies (bell peppers, broccoli, carrots, snap peas)
- 2 cloves garlic, minced
- 1 tablespoon ginger, minced
- 2 tablespoons soy sauce
- 1 tablespoon hoisin sauce
- 1 tablespoon sesame oil
- 1 tablespoon cornstarch
- 1/4 cup water
- Cooked rice or noodles, for serving

Instructions:
1. In a small bowl, whisk together the soy sauce, hoisin sauce, sesame oil, cornstarch, and water to make the stir-fry sauce. Set aside.
2. Heat a tablespoon of oil in a large skillet or wok over medium-high heat. Cook the cubed tofu until golden brown on all sides. Remove the tofu from the skillet and set it aside.
3. In the same skillet, add a little more oil if needed, then add the minced garlic and ginger. Cook for 1 minute until fragrant.
4. Add the mixed vegetables to the skillet and stir-fry for 3-4 minutes until tender-crisp.
5. Return the cooked tofu to the skillet and pour the stir-fry sauce over the tofu and vegetables. Cook for an additional 2-3 minutes until the sauce thickens and coats everything evenly.
6. Serve the tofu and vegetables stir-fried in hot cooked rice or noodles. Enjoy!

Nutritional Information (per serving): Calories: 280, Protein: 20g, Fat: 10g, Carbohydrates: 30g, Fiber: 6g, Calcium: 200mg Cooking Time: 20 minutes

8. **Cottage Cheese Pancakes**

Ingredients:
- 1 cup cottage cheese
- 4 large eggs
- 1/4 cup whole wheat flour
- 1 teaspoon baking powder
- 1 teaspoon vanilla extract
- Maple syrup or honey, for serving
- Fresh berries, for serving

Instructions:
1. In a blender, combine the cottage cheese, eggs, whole wheat flour, baking powder, and vanilla extract. Blend until smooth.
2. Cook in a nonstick skillet or griddle over medium heat. Grease lightly with cooking spray or butter.
3. Pour the pancake batter onto the skillet, using about 1/4 cup of batter for each pancake.
4. Cook the pancakes for 2-3 minutes per side, or until golden brown and fully cooked.

5. Serve the cottage cheese pancakes hot with maple syrup or honey and fresh berries on top. Enjoy!

Nutritional Information (per serving): Calories: 200, Protein: 15g, Fat: 8g, Carbohydrates: 15g, Fiber: 2g, Calcium: 150mg Cooking Time: 15 minutes

9. Almond-Crusted Baked Salmon

Ingredients:
- 4 salmon fillets
- 1/2 cup almond meal or finely ground almonds
- 2 tablespoons grated Parmesan cheese
- 1 teaspoon garlic powder
- 1 teaspoon paprika
- Salt and pepper to taste
- Lemon wedges, for serving

Instructions:
1. Preheat the oven to 400°F (200°C). Line a baking sheet with parchment paper.
2. In a shallow dish, combine the almond meal, Parmesan cheese, garlic powder, paprika, salt, and pepper.
3. Pat the salmon fillets dry with paper towels, then dip each fillet into the almond mixture, pressing gently to coat both sides.
4. Place the coated salmon fillets on the prepared baking sheet.
5. Bake in the preheated oven for 12-15 minutes, or until the salmon is fully cooked and easily flaked with a fork.
6. Serve the almond-crusted baked salmon hot with lemon wedges on the side. Enjoy!

Nutritional Information (per serving): Calories: 300, Protein: 25g, Fat: 20g, Carbohydrates: 5g, Fiber: 2g, Calcium: 150mg Cooking Time: 15 minutes

10. Greek Yogurt Chicken Salad

Ingredients:
- 2 cups cooked chicken breast, shredded or diced.
- 1/2 cup Greek yogurt
- 1/4 cup diced celery
- 1/4 cup diced red onion

- 1/4 cup sliced grapes
- 1/4 cup chopped walnuts
- 1 tablespoon lemon juice
- 1 teaspoon Dijon mustard
- Salt and pepper to taste
- Lettuce leaves, for serving

Instructions:
1. In a large mixing bowl, combine the cooked chicken breast, Greek yogurt, diced celery, diced red onion, sliced grapes, chopped walnuts, lemon juice, Dijon mustard, salt, and pepper. Mix well to combine.
2. Serve the Greek yogurt chicken salad on lettuce leaves as a wrap or over a bed of greens as a salad. Enjoy!

Nutritional Information (per serving): Calories: 250, Protein: 25g, Fat: 10g, Carbohydrates: 10g, Fiber: 2g, Calcium: 150mg Preparation Time: 15 minutes

Chapter 2: Power of Protein

A. Protein's role in bone health

Protein plays a vital role in supporting bone health and integrity. Here's how protein contributes to bone health:

1. Bone Structure: Protein provides the structural framework for bones, contributing to their strength and integrity. Collagen, the most abundant protein in the body, forms the matrix upon which minerals like calcium and phosphorus are deposited, resulting in the formation of dense and resilient bones.

2. Bone Formation and Remodeling: Protein is essential for the process of bone remodeling, which involves the continuous breakdown and formation of bone tissue. Adequate protein intake supports the synthesis of new bone tissue, facilitating bone growth and repair. Without sufficient protein, the body may struggle to maintain bone density and may be more susceptible to fractures and bone loss.

3. Muscle-Bone Interaction: Protein is not only crucial for bone health but also for maintaining muscle mass and strength. Strong muscles provide support and protection to the bones, reducing the risk of falls and fractures. Regular physical activity, combined with adequate protein intake, helps to optimize muscle-bone interaction, promoting overall musculoskeletal health.

4. Calcium Absorption: Protein may also play a role in enhancing calcium absorption in the body. Certain amino acids found in protein-rich foods may facilitate the absorption of calcium from the digestive tract, ensuring that an adequate amount of calcium is available for bone mineralization and maintenance.
5. Hormone Regulation: Protein intake influences the production and activity of hormones that regulate bone metabolism. Hormones such as insulin-like growth factor 1 (IGF-1) and growth hormone play key roles in bone formation and remodeling. Protein-rich diets may support optimal hormone levels, promoting bone health throughout life.

It's important to note that while protein is essential for bone health, excessive protein intake, particularly from animal sources, may have adverse effects on bone health and overall health. A balanced diet that includes a variety of protein sources, such as lean meats, poultry, fish, dairy products, legumes, nuts, and seeds, is recommended for supporting bone health and overall well-being.

B. Protein sources for strong bones

Including protein-rich foods in your diet is essential for supporting bone health and promoting overall well-being. Here are some excellent sources of protein that contribute to strong bones:

1. Lean Meats:
   - Chicken breast
   - Turkey breast
   - Lean cuts of beef (such as sirloin or tenderloin)
   - Pork tenderloin
2. Fatty Fish:
   - Salmon
   - Tuna
   - Mackerel
   - Trout
3. Dairy Products:
   - Greek yogurt
   - Cottage cheese
   - Skim or low-fat milk

- Cheese (such as cheddar, mozzarella, or Swiss)
4. Eggs:
    - Whole eggs
    - Egg whites
5. Plant-Based Proteins:
    - Beans (such as black beans, chickpeas, or lentils)
    - Tofu
    - Tempeh
    - Edamame
6. Nuts and Seeds:
    - Almonds
    - Walnuts
    - Pumpkin seeds
    - Chia seeds
7. Legumes:
    - Lentils
    - Peas
    - Black beans
    - Kidney beans

C. Recipes incorporating protein-rich foods

1. Grilled Salmon with Quinoa Salad

Ingredients:
- 4 salmon fillets
- 1 cup quinoa, cooked
- 1 cup cherry tomatoes, halved
- 1 cucumber, diced
- 1/4 cup red onion, finely chopped
- 1/4 cup fresh parsley, chopped
- Juice of 1 lemon
- 2 tablespoons olive oil
- Salt and pepper to taste

Instructions:
1. Preheat the grill to medium-high heat.

2. Season the salmon fillets with salt, pepper, and a drizzle of olive oil.
3. Grill the salmon fillets for 4-5 minutes per side, or until cooked through and flaky.
4. In a large bowl, combine the cooked quinoa, cherry tomatoes, cucumber, red onion, and parsley.
5. Drizzle the quinoa salad with lemon juice and olive oil. Add salt and pepper to taste.
6. Serve the grilled salmon alongside the quinoa salad. Enjoy!

Nutritional Information (per serving): Calories: 350, Protein: 30g, Fat: 15g, Carbohydrates: 25g, Fiber: 4g, Calcium: 40mg Cooking Time: 15 minutes

2. Black Bean and Sweet Potato Tacos

Ingredients:
- 1 tablespoon olive oil
- 1 onion, diced
- 2 cloves garlic, minced
- 2 cups cooked black beans
- 1 large sweet potato, diced and roasted
- 1 teaspoon ground cumin
- 1 teaspoon chili powder
- Salt and pepper to taste
- 8 small corn or flour tortillas
- Toppings: avocado, salsa, cilantro, lime wedges

Instructions:
1. In a medium-sized skillet, heat the olive oil. Cook the diced onion and minced garlic until softened.
2. Add the cooked black beans, roasted sweet potato, ground cumin, chili powder, salt, and pepper to the skillet. Cook for 5-7 minutes, stirring occasionally, until heated through and well combined.
3. Warm the tortillas in a separate skillet or the oven.
4. Spoon the black bean and sweet potato mixture onto the warm tortillas.
5. Top with sliced avocado, salsa, cilantro, and a squeeze of fresh lime juice.
6. Serve the tacos immediately. Enjoy!

Nutritional Information (per serving): Calories: 300, Protein: 10g, Fat: 8g, Carbohydrates: 50g, Fiber: 10g, Calcium: 80mg Cooking Time: 25 minutes

3. Lentil and Vegetable Curry

Ingredients:
- 1 tablespoon coconut oil
- 1 onion, diced
- 2 cloves garlic, minced
- 1 tablespoon grated ginger
- 2 cups cooked lentils
- 2 cups of chopped vegetables (such as bell peppers, carrots, and zucchini)
- 1 can (14 oz) coconut milk
- 2 tablespoons curry powder
- Salt and pepper to taste
- Cooked rice, for serving
- Fresh cilantro, for garnish

Instructions:
1. Heat the coconut oil in a large skillet or pot over medium heat. Add the diced onion, minced garlic, and grated ginger, and sauté until softened and fragrant.
2. Add the cooked lentils, chopped vegetables, coconut milk, and curry powder to the skillet. Stir to combine.
3. Bring the mixture to a simmer, then reduce heat to low and let it simmer for 15-20 minutes, or until the vegetables are tender and the flavors have melded together.
4. Season the curry with salt and pepper, to taste.
5. Serve the lentil and vegetable curry over cooked rice, garnished with fresh cilantro. Enjoy!

Nutritional Information (per serving): Calories: 320, Protein: 15g, Fat: 10g, Carbohydrates: 45g, Fiber: 10g, Calcium: 70mg Cooking Time: 30 minutes

4. Chicken and Quinoa Stuffed Bell Peppers

Ingredients:
- 4 large bell peppers, halved and seeded
- 1 cup cooked quinoa
- 1 cup cooked chicken breast, diced
- 1/2 cup of rinsed and drained black beans

- 1/2 cup corn kernels
- 1/2 cup diced tomatoes
- 1/4 cup chopped fresh cilantro
- 1 teaspoon cumin
- 1 teaspoon chili powder
- Salt and pepper to taste
- 1/2 cup shredded cheddar cheese (optional)
- Sliced avocado, for serving (optional)

Instructions:
1. Preheat the oven to 375°F (190°C). Place the halved bell peppers in a baking dish.
2. In a large mixing bowl, combine the cooked quinoa, diced chicken breast, black beans, corn kernels, diced tomatoes, chopped cilantro, cumin, chili powder, salt, and pepper.
3. Spoon the quinoa and chicken mixture into each bell pepper half, pressing down gently to fill.
4. If desired, sprinkle shredded cheddar cheese on top of each stuffed pepper.
5. Cover the baking dish with aluminum foil and bake in the preheated oven for 25-30 minutes, or until the peppers are tender.
6. Remove the foil and bake for an additional 5 minutes to melt the cheese, if using.
7. Serve the stuffed bell peppers hot, garnished with sliced avocado if desired. Enjoy!

Nutritional Information (per serving): Calories: 300, Protein: 20g, Fat: 8g, Carbohydrates: 35g, Fiber: 8g, Calcium: 100mg Cooking Time: 40 minutes

5. **Turkey and Spinach Meatballs**

Ingredients:
- 1 lb ground turkey
- 1 cup fresh spinach, finely chopped
- 1/4 cup grated Parmesan cheese
- 1/4 cup breadcrumbs
- 1 egg
- 2 cloves garlic, minced
- 1 teaspoon Italian seasoning

- Salt and pepper to taste
- Olive oil for cooking

Instructions:
1. Preheat the oven to 375°F (190°C). Line a baking sheet with parchment paper.
2. In a large mixing bowl, combine the ground turkey, chopped spinach, grated Parmesan cheese, breadcrumbs, egg, minced garlic, Italian seasoning, salt, and pepper. Mix until well combined.
3. Shape the mixture into golf ball-sized meatballs and place them on the prepared baking sheet.
4. Drizzle or spray the meatballs with olive oil.
5. Bake in the preheated oven for 20-25 minutes, or until the meatballs are thoroughly cooked and golden brown.
6. Serve the turkey and spinach meatballs hot with your favorite sauce or over pasta. Enjoy!

Nutritional Information (per serving): Calories: 250, Protein: 25g, Fat: 10g, Carbohydrates: 10g, Fiber: 2g, Calcium: 50mg Cooking Time: 25 minutes

6. **Quinoa-Stuffed Bell Peppers**

Ingredients:
- 4 bell peppers, halved and seeded
- 1 cup quinoa, cooked
- 1 can (15 oz) black beans, rinsed and drained
- 1 cup corn kernels
- 1 cup diced tomatoes
- 1 teaspoon chili powder
- 1 teaspoon cumin
- Salt and pepper to taste
- 1/2 cup shredded cheddar cheese (optional)

Instructions:
1. Preheat the oven to 375°F (190°C).
2. In a large bowl, combine cooked quinoa, black beans, corn kernels, diced tomatoes, chili powder, cumin, salt, and pepper.
3. Stuff each bell pepper half with the quinoa mixture and place them in a baking dish.

4. If desired, sprinkle shredded cheddar cheese over the stuffed bell peppers.
5. Cover the baking dish with foil and bake for 25-30 minutes, or until the peppers are tender.
6. Remove the foil and bake for an additional 5 minutes to melt the cheese (if using).
7. Serve hot and enjoy!

Nutritional Information (per serving): Calories: 250, Protein: 12g, Fat: 5g, Carbohydrates: 45g, Fiber: 10g, Calcium: 100mg Cooking Time: 40 minutes

7. **Chickpea and Vegetable Stir-Fry**

Ingredients:
- 1 tablespoon sesame oil
- 1 onion, sliced
- 2 cloves garlic, minced
- 1 bell pepper, sliced
- 1 cup sliced mushrooms
- 1 can (15 oz) chickpeas, rinsed and drained
- 2 cups broccoli florets
- 2 tablespoons soy sauce
- 1 tablespoon rice vinegar
- 1 tablespoon honey or maple syrup
- 1 teaspoon ginger, grated
- Cooked rice or noodles, for serving

Instructions:
1. Heat sesame oil in a large skillet or wok over medium-high heat.
2. Add sliced onion and minced garlic to the skillet and cook until fragrant.
3. Add sliced bell pepper and mushrooms to the skillet and stir-fry for 3-4 minutes.
4. Stir in chickpeas and broccoli florets, and cook for an additional 3-4 minutes.
5. In a small bowl, whisk together soy sauce, rice vinegar, honey or maple syrup, and grated ginger.
6. Pour the sauce over the chickpea and vegetable mixture into the skillet. Stir well to coat.

7. Cook for another 2-3 minutes until the sauce thickens and the vegetables are tender.
8. Serve the stir-fried hot cooked rice or noodles. Enjoy!

Nutritional Information (per serving): Calories: 280, Protein: 10g, Fat: 7g, Carbohydrates: 45g, Fiber: 10g, Calcium: 80mg Cooking Time: 20 minutes

8. **Chicken and Quinoa Salad**

Ingredients:
- 2 cups cooked quinoa
- 2 cups cooked chicken breast, shredded
- 1 cup cherry tomatoes, halved
- 1 cucumber, diced
- 1/4 cup red onion, finely chopped
- 1/4 cup fresh parsley, chopped
- Juice of 1 lemon
- 2 tablespoons olive oil
- Salt and pepper to taste

Instructions:
1. In a large mixing bowl, combine cooked quinoa, cooked chicken breast, cherry tomatoes, cucumber, red onion, and parsley.
2. Toss the salad with lemon juice and olive oil. Add salt and pepper to taste.
3. Toss everything together until well combined.
4. Serve the chicken and quinoa salad chilled or at room temperature. Enjoy!

Nutritional Information (per serving): Calories: 300, Protein: 25g, Fat: 10g, Carbohydrates: 25g, Fiber: 4g, Calcium: 50mg Preparation Time: 15 minutes

9. **Eggplant Parmesan**

Ingredients:
- 1 large eggplant, sliced into rounds
- 2 eggs, beaten
- 1 cup breadcrumbs
- 1 cup marinara sauce
- 1 cup shredded mozzarella cheese
- 1/4 cup grated Parmesan cheese
- Fresh basil leaves, for garnish

- Salt and pepper to taste

Instructions:
1. Preheat the oven to 375°F (190°C). Line a baking sheet with parchment paper.
2. Dip eggplant slices into beaten eggs, then coat with breadcrumbs. Place them on the prepared baking sheet.
3. Bake the eggplant slices in the preheated oven for 20-25 minutes, or until golden brown and crispy.
4. Remove the baked eggplant slices from the oven and spread the marinara sauce on top of each slice.
5. Sprinkle shredded mozzarella cheese and grated Parmesan cheese over the marinara sauce.
6. Return the baking sheet to the oven and bake for an additional 10-15 minutes, or until the cheese is melted and bubbly.
7. Garnish with fresh basil leaves before serving. Enjoy!

Nutritional Information (per serving): Calories: 280, Protein: 12g, Fat: 10g, Carbohydrates: 35g, Fiber: 8g, Calcium: 150mg Cooking Time: 45 minutes

Chapter 3: Essential Nutrients for Bone Health

A. Overview of other important nutrients

In addition to protein, several other nutrients play vital roles in supporting bone health and overall well-being. Here's an overview of some key nutrients and their importance:

1. Calcium: Calcium is essential for building and maintaining strong bones and teeth. It also plays an important role in muscle function, nerve transmission, and blood clotting. Incorporating calcium-rich foods into your diet, such as dairy products, leafy greens, nuts, and fortified foods, can help meet your daily calcium needs.
2. Vitamin D: Vitamin D is necessary for the absorption of calcium and phosphate, which are important minerals for bone health. Vitamin D can be obtained from foods such as fatty fish, fortified dairy products, and egg yolks, as well as from sunlight. Vitamin D supplementation may be required for people who get little sun or are at risk of deficiency.
3. Vitamin K: Vitamin K plays a role in bone metabolism and helps regulate calcium deposition in bone tissue. Green leafy vegetables, broccoli, Brussels sprouts, and fermented foods like sauerkraut are good sources of vitamin K.
4. Magnesium: Magnesium is involved in bone formation and supports the structural integrity of bone tissue. It also contributes to muscle and nerve

function, energy production, and protein synthesis. Nuts, seeds, whole grains, legumes, and leafy greens are excellent sources of magnesium.
5. Phosphorus: Phosphorus works alongside calcium to strengthen bones and teeth. It is found in abundance in protein-rich foods such as meat, poultry, fish, dairy products, nuts, and seeds.
6. Vitamin C is essential for collagen synthesis, a structural component of bones, cartilage, and connective tissue. Citrus fruits, strawberries, kiwi, bell peppers, and broccoli are rich sources of vitamin C.
7. Zinc: Zinc aids in bone mineralization, immune function, and wound healing. Good sources of zinc include oysters, red meat, poultry, beans, nuts, and whole grains.
8. Omega-3 fatty acids are anti-inflammatory and may help lower the risk of osteoporosis by increasing bone density and strength. Fatty fish such as salmon, mackerel, and sardines are excellent sources of omega-3s.

B. List of foods rich in magnesium, phosphorus, and vitamin K

Here's a list of foods that are excellent sources of magnesium, phosphorus, and vitamin K:

1. Magnesium-Rich Foods:
   - Nuts (almonds, cashews, peanuts)
   - Seeds (pumpkin seeds, sunflower seeds, flaxseeds, chia seeds)
   - Whole grains (brown rice, oats, quinoa, whole wheat)
   - Legumes (black beans, chickpeas, lentils)
   - Leafy greens (spinach, kale, Swiss chard)
   - Avocado
   - Bananas
   - Dark chocolate
2. Phosphorus-Rich Foods:
   - Dairy products (milk, yogurt, cheese)
   - Meat (beef, pork, chicken, turkey)
   - Fish (salmon, tuna, mackerel)
   - Seafood (oysters, clams, shrimp)
   - Eggs
   - Nuts and seeds (pumpkin seeds, sesame seeds)

- Legumes (lentils, chickpeas, black beans)
- Whole grains (brown rice, whole wheat bread, barley)
3. Vitamin K-Rich Foods:
    - leafy greens (kale, spinach, collard greens, Swiss chard)
    - Cruciferous vegetables (broccoli, Brussels sprouts, cabbage)
    - Herbs (parsley, basil, cilantro)
    - Green vegetables (asparagus, green beans, peas)
    - Brussels sprouts
    - Fermented foods (sauerkraut, kimchi)
    - Natto (fermented soybeans)
    - Spring onions (scallions)

C. Recipes featuring these essential nutrients

1. Kale and Quinoa Salad with Almonds and Dried Cranberries

Ingredients:
- 2 cups cooked quinoa
- 4 cups chopped kale leaves
- 1/2 cup sliced almonds
- 1/2 cup dried cranberries
- 1/4 cup lemon juice
- 2 tablespoons olive oil
- Salt and pepper to taste

Instructions:
1. In a large bowl, combine cooked quinoa, chopped kale leaves, sliced almonds, and dried cranberries.
2. Drizzle the salad with lemon juice and olive oil. Add salt and pepper to taste.
3. Toss everything together until well combined.
4. Serve the kale and quinoa salad chilled or at room temperature. Enjoy!

Nutritional Information (per serving): Calories: 300, Protein: 8g, Fat: 12g, Carbohydrates: 40g, Fiber: 6g, Calcium: 100mg Preparation Time: 15 minutes

2. Sesame-crusted Tofu Stir-Fry

Ingredients:
- 1 block (14 ounces) of firm tofu, drained and cubed
- 2 tablespoons soy sauce
- 1 tablespoon sesame oil
- 1 tablespoon cornstarch
- 2 tablespoons sesame seeds
- 1 tablespoon olive oil
- 2 cups mixed vegetables (bell peppers, broccoli, carrots)
- Cooked rice, for serving
- Green onions, for garnish

Instructions:
1. In a bowl, combine cubed tofu, soy sauce, sesame oil, and cornstarch. Toss until tofu is evenly coated.
2. Sprinkle sesame seeds over the tofu and gently press to adhere.
3. Heat the olive oil in a large skillet or wok over medium-high heat. Add tofu cubes and cook until golden brown and crispy on all sides.
4. Stir-fry the mixed vegetables in the skillet until they are tender and crispy.
5. Serve the sesame-crusted tofu and mixed vegetables over cooked rice. Garnish with sliced green onions. Enjoy!

Nutritional Information (per serving): Calories: 350, Protein: 20g, Fat: 18g, Carbohydrates: 30g, Fiber: 6g, Calcium: 200mg Cooking Time: 25 minutes

3. Baked Sweet Potato Fries with Garlic Aioli

Ingredients:
- 2 large sweet potatoes, cut into fries
- 2 tablespoons olive oil
- 1 teaspoon paprika
- 1/2 teaspoon garlic powder
- Salt and pepper to taste
- For Garlic Aioli:
    - 1/2 cup mayonnaise
    - 2 cloves garlic, minced
    - 1 tablespoon lemon juice
    - Salt and pepper to taste

Instructions:
1. Preheat the oven to 425°F (220°C). Line a baking sheet with parchment paper.
2. In a bowl, toss sweet potato fries with olive oil, paprika, garlic powder, salt, and pepper until evenly coated.
3. Spread the seasoned sweet potato fries in a single layer on the prepared baking sheet.
4. Bake in the preheated oven for 25-30 minutes, flipping halfway through, until fries are golden and crispy.
5. While the fries are baking, prepare the garlic aioli by combining mayonnaise, minced garlic, lemon juice, salt, and pepper in a small bowl. Mix well.
6. Serve the baked sweet potato fries hot with garlic aioli for dipping. Enjoy!

Nutritional Information (per serving): Calories: 250, Protein: 2g, Fat: 18g, Carbohydrates: 20g, Fiber: 3g, Calcium: 40mg Cooking Time: 30 minutes

4. **Salmon and Broccoli Sheet Pan Dinner**

Ingredients:
- 4 salmon fillets
- 4 cups broccoli florets
- 2 tablespoons olive oil
- 2 cloves garlic, minced
- 1 teaspoon lemon zest
- 1 tablespoon lemon juice
- Salt and pepper to taste

Instructions:
1. Preheat the oven to 400°F (200°C). Line a baking sheet with parchment paper.
2. Place salmon fillets and broccoli florets on the prepared baking sheet.
3. In a small bowl, whisk together olive oil, minced garlic, lemon zest, lemon juice, salt, and pepper.
4. Drizzle the olive oil mixture over the salmon and broccoli, tossing to coat evenly.
5. Arrange the salmon fillets skin-side down and spread the broccoli florets in a single layer.

6. Bake in a preheated oven for 15-20 minutes, or until the salmon is fully cooked and the broccoli is tender.
7. Serve the salmon and broccoli hot, garnished with additional lemon slices if desired. Enjoy!

Nutritional Information (per serving): Calories: 300, Protein: 25g, Fat: 15g, Carbohydrates: 10g, Fiber: 4g, Calcium: 100mg Cooking Time: 20 minutes

5. Spinach and Feta Stuffed Chicken Breast

Ingredients:
- 4 boneless, skinless chicken breasts
- 2 cups fresh spinach leaves
- 1/2 cup crumbled feta cheese
- 2 cloves garlic, minced
- 1 tablespoon olive oil
- Salt and pepper to taste
- Toothpicks or kitchen twine

Instructions:
1. Preheat the oven to 375°F (190°C). Grease a baking dish with olive oil.
2. Using a sharp knife, cut a pocket into each chicken breast, being careful not to cut all the way through.
3. In a skillet, heat olive oil over medium heat. Add minced garlic and cook until fragrant.
4. Cook the fresh spinach leaves in the skillet until wilted. Remove from heat and allow to cool slightly.
5. Once cooled, mix in the crumbled feta cheese.
6. Stuff each chicken breast with the spinach and feta mixture, then secure with toothpicks or tie with kitchen twine to keep the filling inside.
7. Place stuffed chicken breasts in the prepared baking dish—season with salt and pepper.
8. Bake in the preheated oven for 25-30 minutes, or until the chicken is cooked through and juices run clear.
9. Remove toothpicks or kitchen twine before serving. Enjoy!

Nutritional Information (per serving): Calories: 300, Protein: 35g, Fat: 15g, Carbohydrates: 5g, Fiber: 2g, Calcium: 150mg Cooking Time: 30 minutes

6. Greek Yogurt Parfait with Berries and Almonds

Ingredients:
- 2 cups Greek yogurt
- 1 cup mixed berries (such as strawberries, blueberries, or raspberries)
- 1/4 cup almonds, chopped
- 2 tablespoons honey or maple syrup
- 1 teaspoon vanilla extract

Instructions:
1. In a small bowl, mix Greek yogurt with honey or maple syrup and vanilla extract until well combined.
2. Layer Greek yogurt mixture, mixed berries, and chopped almonds in serving glasses or bowls.
3. Repeat the layers until all of the ingredients have been used, then top with berries and almonds.
4. Serve the Greek yogurt parfait immediately as a nutritious breakfast or snack. Enjoy!

Nutritional Information (per serving): Calories: 250, Protein: 20g, Fat: 10g, Carbohydrates: 25g, Fiber: 5g, Calcium: 200mg Preparation Time: 10 minutes

7. Black Bean and Corn Salad with Avocado

Ingredients:
- 1 can (15 oz) of black beans, rinsed and drained
- 1 cup corn kernels (fresh, frozen, or canned)
- 1 avocado, diced
- 1/4 cup red onion, finely chopped
- 1/4 cup fresh cilantro, chopped
- Juice of 1 lime
- 2 tablespoons olive oil
- Salt and pepper to taste

Instructions:
1. In a large bowl, combine black beans, corn kernels, diced avocado, chopped red onion, and chopped cilantro.
2. Drizzle lime juice and olive oil over the salad. Add salt and pepper to taste.
3. Toss everything together until well combined.

4. Serve the black bean and corn salad as a side dish or as a topping for tacos or grilled meats. Enjoy!

Nutritional Information (per serving): Calories: 300, Protein: 10g, Fat: 15g, Carbohydrates: 35g, Fiber: 12g, Calcium: 80mg Preparation Time: 15 minutes

8. **Grilled Vegetable Quinoa Bowls**

Ingredients:
- 1 cup quinoa, rinsed and drained
- 2 cups water or vegetable broth
- 2 bell peppers, sliced
- 1 zucchini, sliced
- 1 yellow squash, sliced
- 1 red onion, sliced
- 2 tablespoons olive oil
- Salt and pepper to taste
- 1/4 cup fresh basil leaves, chopped
- Balsamic glaze for drizzling (optional)

Instructions:
1. Heat water or vegetable broth in a medium saucepan until it boils. Reduce the heat to low, cover, and simmer for 15-20 minutes, or until the quinoa is cooked and the water has been absorbed; fluff with a fork and set aside.
2. Preheat the grill to medium-high heat.
3. In a large bowl, toss sliced bell peppers, zucchini, yellow squash, and red onion with olive oil, salt, and pepper until evenly coated.
4. Grill the vegetables for 5-7 minutes per side, or until they are tender and have grill marks.
5. To assemble the bowls, divide cooked quinoa among serving bowls. Garnish with grilled vegetables and chopped basil leaves. Drizzle with balsamic glaze if desired.
6. Serve the grilled vegetable quinoa bowls hot and enjoy!

Nutritional Information (per serving): Calories: 300, Protein: 8g, Fat: 10g, Carbohydrates: 45g, Fiber: 8g, Calcium: 60mg Cooking Time: 30 minutes

9. Turkey and Quinoa Stuffed Bell Peppers

Ingredients:
- 4 bell peppers, halved and seeded
- 1 cup quinoa, rinsed and drained
- 1 pound ground turkey
- 1 onion, diced
- 2 cloves garlic, minced
- 1 can (15 oz) diced tomatoes
- 1 teaspoon dried oregano
- 1 teaspoon dried basil
- Salt and pepper to taste
- 1/2 cup shredded mozzarella cheese

Instructions:
1. Preheat oven to 375°F (190°C). Grease a baking dish with olive oil.
2. In a large skillet, cook ground turkey over medium heat until browned. Add diced onion and minced garlic, and cook until softened.
3. Stir in cooked quinoa, diced tomatoes, dried oregano, dried basil, salt, and pepper. Cook for an additional 5 minutes, then remove from heat.
4. Fill the bell pepper halves with the turkey and quinoa mixture. Place them in the baking dish that you've prepared.
5. Cover the dish with foil and bake in the preheated oven for 25-30 minutes, or until peppers are tender.
6. Remove foil, sprinkle shredded mozzarella cheese over the stuffed peppers, and bake for an additional 5 minutes, or until cheese is melted and bubbly.
7. Serve the turkey and quinoa stuffed bell peppers hot. Enjoy!

Nutritional Information (per serving): Calories: 350, Protein: 25g, Fat: 15g, Carbohydrates: 30g, Fiber: 6g, Calcium: 100mg Cooking Time: 45 minutes

Chapter 4: Fortifying with Fruits and Vegetables

A. Antioxidants and phytonutrients for bone health

Antioxidants and phytonutrients are essential for maintaining bone health by protecting against oxidative stress and inflammation, which can contribute to bone loss and weaken bone structure. Here's an overview of some antioxidants and phytonutrients that support bone health:

1. **Vitamin C**: Ascorbic acid, commonly known as vitamin C, is a powerful antioxidant that plays a crucial role in collagen synthesis, which is important for maintaining the integrity of bones, cartilage, and connective tissues.
2. **Vitamin E**: Vitamin E is a fat-soluble antioxidant that helps protect cells from oxidative damage. It may also have anti-inflammatory properties that can support bone health by reducing inflammation and promoting bone formation.
3. **Flavonoids**: Flavonoids are a group of phytonutrients found in fruits, vegetables, and other plant-based foods. They have antioxidant and anti-inflammatory properties that can help protect bone cells from damage and support bone density.
4. **Polyphenols**: Polyphenols are another group of phytonutrients with antioxidant properties found in foods such as berries, tea, cocoa, and nuts.

They may help reduce bone loss by inhibiting the activity of osteoclasts, the cells responsible for breaking down bone tissue.
5. **Carotenoids**: Carotenoids are pigments found in colorful fruits and vegetables, such as carrots, sweet potatoes, spinach, and tomatoes. Some carotenoids, such as beta-carotene and lycopene, have antioxidant properties that can help protect bone cells and support bone health.
6. **Isoflavones**: Isoflavones are phytoestrogens found in soybeans and soy products. They have been shown to have estrogen-like effects on the body, which may help reduce bone loss and maintain bone density, especially in postmenopausal women.
7. **Resveratrol**: Resveratrol is a polyphenol found in red wine, grapes, and berries. It has been studied for its potential to promote bone health by reducing inflammation and oxidative stress, as well as stimulating bone formation

B. Fruits and vegetables to include in the diet

Including a variety of fruits and vegetables in your diet is essential for supporting bone health and overall well-being. Here are some nutrient-rich options to consider incorporating into your meals:
1. **Leafy Greens**: Spinach, kale, collard greens, Swiss chard, and beet greens are excellent sources of calcium, vitamin K, and other bone-building nutrients.
2. **Broccoli**: Broccoli is rich in calcium, vitamin C, and vitamin K, making it a great choice for supporting bone health and reducing the risk of osteoporosis.
3. **Berries**: Blueberries, strawberries, raspberries, and blackberries are packed with antioxidants, including vitamin C and flavonoids, which help protect bone cells from damage.
4. **Citrus Fruits**: Oranges, grapefruits, lemons, and limes are rich in vitamin C, which is important for collagen synthesis and bone formation.
5. **Tomatoes**: Tomatoes are a good source of lycopene, a powerful antioxidant that may help reduce the risk of osteoporosis and protect bone health.
6. **Sweet Potatoes**: Sweet potatoes are high in beta-carotene, vitamin C, and potassium, which are beneficial for bone health and overall wellness.

7. **Bell Peppers**: Bell peppers are rich in vitamin C and other antioxidants that help support bone health and reduce inflammation.
8. **Avocado**: Avocado is a nutrient-dense fruit that provides potassium, vitamin K, vitamin E, and other essential nutrients for bone health.
9. **Cruciferous Vegetables**: Cauliflower, Brussels sprouts, cabbage, and bok choy are rich in vitamins, minerals, and phytonutrients that support bone health.
10. **Bananas**: Bananas are a good source of potassium, which helps maintain bone density and prevent muscle cramps.
11. **Apples**: Apples contain quercetin, a flavonoid that may help reduce inflammation and protect bone health.
12. **Grapes**: Grapes contain resveratrol, a polyphenol with antioxidant properties that may help protect bone cells and reduce the risk of osteoporosis.

C. Recipes highlighting colorful produce

1. **Roasted Vegetable Medley with Balsamic Glaze**

Ingredients:
- 2 cups mixed vegetables (such as bell peppers, zucchini, cherry tomatoes, red onion)
- 2 tablespoons olive oil
- Salt and pepper to taste
- 2 tablespoons balsamic glaze

Instructions:
1. Preheat the oven to 400°F (200°C).
2. Cut the mixed vegetables into bite-sized pieces and place them on a baking sheet.
3. Drizzle olive oil over the vegetables and season with salt and pepper. Toss to coat evenly.
4. Roast the vegetables in the preheated oven for 20-25 minutes, or until tender and caramelized.
5. Remove from the oven and drizzle with balsamic glaze before serving.
6. Serve the roasted vegetable medley as a colorful and flavorful side dish. Enjoy!

Nutritional Information (per serving): Calories: 150, Protein: 2g, Fat: 8g, Carbohydrates: 18g, Fiber: 5g, Calcium: 40mg Cooking Time: 25 minutes

2. Mixed Berry Smoothie Bowl

Ingredients:
- 1 cup mixed berries (such as strawberries, blueberries, or raspberries)
- 1 ripe banana
- 1/2 cup Greek yogurt
- 1/4 cup of almond milk (or any milk of your choice)
- 1 tablespoon honey or maple syrup (optional)
- Toppings: granola, sliced almonds, shredded coconut, chia seeds, sliced fruit

Instructions:
1. In a blender, combine mixed berries, banana, Greek yogurt, almond milk, and honey or maple syrup (if using). Blend until smooth and creamy.
2. Pour the smoothie into a bowl and top with granola, sliced almonds, shredded coconut, chia seeds, and sliced fruit.
3. Customize your smoothie bowl with your favorite toppings and enjoy immediately!

Nutritional Information (per serving): Calories: 250, Protein: 10g, Fat: 6g, Carbohydrates: 40g, Fiber: 8g, Calcium: 150mg Preparation Time: 10 minutes

3. Stuffed Bell Peppers with Quinoa and Chickpeas

Ingredients:
- 4 bell peppers, halved and seeded
- 1 cup cooked quinoa
- 1 can (15 oz) chickpeas, rinsed and drained
- 1 cup cherry tomatoes, halved
- 1/2 cup feta cheese, crumbled
- 2 tablespoons olive oil
- 1 teaspoon dried oregano
- Salt and pepper to taste

Instructions:
1. Preheat the oven to 375°F (190°C). Grease a baking dish with olive oil.
2. In a large bowl, combine cooked quinoa, chickpeas, cherry tomatoes, feta cheese, olive oil, dried oregano, salt, and pepper.

3. Spoon the quinoa mixture into each halved bell pepper, filling them evenly.
4. Place stuffed bell peppers in the prepared baking dish. Cover with foil and bake for 25 to 30 minutes.
5. Remove foil and bake for an additional 5 minutes, or until the peppers are tender and the filling is heated through.
6. Serve the stuffed bell peppers hot, garnished with fresh herbs if desired. Enjoy!

Nutritional Information (per serving): Calories: 300, Protein: 12g, Fat: 12g, Carbohydrates: 35g, Fiber: 8g, Calcium: 120mg Cooking Time: 35 minutes

4. **Rainbow Veggie Stir-Fry**

Ingredients:
- 2 cups mixed bell peppers, sliced (red, yellow, green)
- 1 cup broccoli florets
- 1 cup snow peas, trimmed
- 1 cup carrots, julienned
- 1 cup cherry tomatoes, halved
- 2 tablespoons olive oil
- 2 cloves garlic, minced
- 1 tablespoon soy sauce or tamari
- 1 tablespoon rice vinegar
- Salt and pepper to taste
- Cooked rice or noodles, for serving

Instructions:
1. Heat the olive oil in a large skillet or wok over medium-high heat. Add the minced garlic and cook until fragrant.
2. Add mixed bell peppers, broccoli florets, snow peas, and carrots to the skillet. Stir-fry for 4-5 minutes, or until vegetables are tender-crisp.
3. Add cherry tomatoes to the skillet and cook for an additional 1-2 minutes.
4. Drizzle soy sauce and rice vinegar over the stir-fried vegetables. Season with salt and pepper to taste. Toss everything together until well combined.
5. Serve the rainbow veggie stir-fry over cooked rice or noodles. Enjoy!

Nutritional Information (per serving): Calories: 200, Protein: 5g, Fat: 8g, Carbohydrates: 25g, Fiber: 6g, Calcium: 60mg Cooking Time: 15 minutes

5. **Mango and Avocado Salad with Citrus Dressing**

Ingredients:
- 2 cups mixed salad greens (spinach, arugula, kale)
- 1 ripe mango, diced
- 1 ripe avocado, diced
- 1/4 cup red onion, thinly sliced
- 1/4 cup toasted almonds, chopped

For Citrus Dressing:
- Juice of 1 lime
- Juice of 1 orange
- 2 tablespoons olive oil
- 1 teaspoon honey or maple syrup
- Salt and pepper to taste

Instructions:
1. In a large salad bowl, combine mixed salad greens, diced mango, diced avocado, thinly sliced red onion, and chopped toasted almonds.
2. In a small bowl, whisk together lime juice, orange juice, olive oil, honey or maple syrup, salt, and pepper to make the citrus dressing.
3. Drizzle the citrus dressing over the salad and toss gently to coat all the ingredients.
4. Serve the mango and avocado salad immediately as a refreshing side dish or light meal. Enjoy!

Nutritional Information (per serving): Calories: 250, Protein: 5g, Fat: 15g, Carbohydrates: 30g, Fiber: 8g, Calcium: 70mg Preparation Time: 15 minutes

Chapter 5: Healthy Fats for Strong Bones

A. Importance of omega-3 fatty acids

Omega-3 fatty acids are a group of essential fatty acids that are vital for overall health, including bone health. Here are some key reasons why omega-3 fatty acids are important:

1. **Bone Health**: Omega-3 fatty acids have been shown to help maintain bone density and reduce the risk of osteoporosis, a condition characterized by fragile and brittle bones. They can also help decrease inflammation in the body, which is linked to bone loss and osteoporosis.
2. **Anti-Inflammatory Properties**: Omega-3 fatty acids have powerful anti-inflammatory effects on the body. Chronic inflammation is associated with various health conditions, including osteoporosis, arthritis, and cardiovascular disease. By reducing inflammation, omega-3 fatty acids can help protect against bone loss and maintain bone health.
3. **Enhanced Calcium Absorption**: Omega-3 fatty acids may enhance the absorption of calcium in the body, which is essential for building and maintaining strong bones and teeth. Adequate calcium intake, along with omega-3 fatty acids, can help support optimal bone health.
4. **Bone Mineralization**: Omega-3 fatty acids play a role in bone mineralization, the process by which minerals such as calcium and phosphorus are deposited into bone tissue, strengthening the bones and preventing fractures.
5. **Joint Health**: Omega-3 fatty acids can help reduce joint pain and stiffness associated with conditions such as arthritis. Maintaining joint health is important for overall mobility and quality of life, especially as we age.
6. **Heart Health**: Omega-3 fatty acids are well-known for their cardiovascular benefits, including reducing the risk of heart disease and lowering levels of triglycerides in the blood. A healthy heart is essential for delivering nutrients and oxygen to the bones, supporting bone health indirectly.
7. **Brain Health**: Omega-3 fatty acids, particularly DHA (docosahexaenoic acid), are important for brain development and function. A healthy brain is essential for regulating various bodily functions, including bone metabolism.

B. Sources of healthy fats

Including healthy fats in your diet is important for overall health, including bone health. Here are some sources of healthy fats to incorporate into your meals:

1. **Fatty Fish**: Fatty fish such as salmon, mackerel, trout, sardines, and herring are rich in omega-3 fatty acids, which have numerous health benefits, including supporting heart health and reducing inflammation. Aim to include fatty fish in your diet at least twice a week.
2. **Avocado**: Avocado is a nutritious fruit that is rich in monounsaturated fats, particularly oleic acid. It also contains fiber, vitamins, and minerals, making it a versatile and healthy addition to salads, sandwiches, smoothies, and more.
3. **Nuts and Seeds**: Nuts and seeds are excellent sources of healthy fats, protein, fiber, vitamins, and minerals. Some of the best options include almonds, walnuts, pistachios, pecans, chia seeds, flaxseeds, hemp seeds, and pumpkin seeds. Enjoy them as a snack, sprinkle them on salads or yogurt, or use them to make nut butter or seed butter.
4. **Olives and Olive Oil**: Olives and extra virgin olive oil are rich in monounsaturated fats, particularly oleic acid, as well as antioxidants and anti-inflammatory compounds. Use olive oil for cooking, salad dressings, and marinades, and enjoy olives as a snack or as part of Mediterranean-inspired dishes.
5. **Coconut and Coconut Oil**: Coconut and coconut oil contain medium-chain triglycerides (MCTs), which are metabolized differently in the body compared to other types of fats. Coconut oil is suitable for cooking at high temperatures and can add flavor to both sweet and savory dishes.
6. **Flaxseeds and Flaxseed Oil**: Flaxseeds and flaxseed oil are rich in alpha-linolenic acid (ALA), a type of omega-3 fatty acid. Ground flaxseeds can be sprinkled on oatmeal, yogurt, or smoothies, while flaxseed oil can be used in salad dressings or added to cooked dishes.
7. **Chia Seeds**: Chia seeds are another excellent source of healthy fats, particularly ALA omega-3 fatty acids. They are also rich in fiber, protein, and various vitamins and minerals. Chia seeds can be soaked in water or milk to make chia pudding, added to smoothies, or used as a topping for yogurt or oatmeal.

8. **Walnuts**: Walnuts are one of the best plant-based sources of omega-3 fatty acids, particularly ALA. They are also rich in antioxidants and provide a satisfying crunch to salads, baked goods, and oatmeal.

C. Recipes featuring omega-3-rich ingredients

1. Avocado and Chickpea Salad

Ingredients:
- 2 ripe avocados, diced
- 1 can (15 oz) chickpeas, rinsed and drained
- 1 cup cherry tomatoes, halved
- 1/4 cup red onion, finely chopped
- 2 tablespoons fresh cilantro, chopped
- Juice of 1 lime
- 2 tablespoons extra virgin olive oil
- Salt and pepper to taste

Instructions:
1. In a large salad bowl, combine diced avocados, chickpeas, cherry tomatoes, red onion, and chopped cilantro.
2. Drizzle lime juice and olive oil over the salad. Season with salt and pepper as desired.
3. Toss gently until everything is well combined.
4. Serve the avocado and chickpea salad as a refreshing side dish or light meal. Enjoy!

Nutritional Information (per serving): Calories: 250, Protein: 6g, Fat: 15g, Carbohydrates: 25g, Fiber: 10g, Calcium: 50mg Preparation Time: 10 minutes

2. Walnut-Crusted Chicken Breast

Ingredients:
- 4 boneless, skinless chicken breasts
- 1 cup walnuts, finely chopped
- 2 tablespoons whole wheat flour
- 1 teaspoon paprika
- 1 teaspoon garlic powder
- 1/2 teaspoon salt

- 1/4 teaspoon black pepper
- 2 eggs, beaten
- 2 tablespoons olive oil

Instructions:
1. Preheat the oven to 375°F (190°C). Grease a baking dish with olive oil.
2. In a shallow dish, combine finely chopped walnuts, whole wheat flour, paprika, garlic powder, salt, and black pepper.
3. Dip each chicken breast in the beaten eggs, then coat with the walnut mixture, pressing gently to adhere.
4. Place the coated chicken breasts in the prepared baking dish. Drizzle with olive oil.
5. Bake in the preheated oven for 25-30 minutes, or until the chicken is cooked through and the walnut crust is golden brown.
6. Serve the walnut-crusted chicken breast hot with your favorite side dishes. Enjoy!

Nutritional Information (per serving): Calories: 350, Protein: 30g, Fat: 20g, Carbohydrates: 10g, Fiber: 3g, Calcium: 40mg Cooking Time: 30 minutes

3. **Grilled Veggie and Hummus Wrap**

Ingredients:
- 4 whole wheat tortillas
- 1 cup mixed grilled vegetables (bell peppers, zucchini, eggplant)
- 1/2 cup hummus
- 1/4 cup crumbled feta cheese
- Fresh spinach leaves

Instructions:
1. Heat the whole wheat tortillas on a grill or stovetop until warm and slightly toasted.
2. Spread a generous amount of hummus on each tortilla.
3. Top with mixed grilled vegetables, crumbled feta cheese, and fresh spinach leaves.
4. Roll up the tortillas tightly to form wraps.
5. Serve the grilled veggie and hummus wraps immediately as a delicious and nutritious meal. Enjoy!

Nutritional Information (per serving): Calories: 300, Protein: 8g, Fat: 12g, Carbohydrates: 40g, Fiber: 8g, Calcium: 80mg Preparation Time: 20 minutes

4. **Salmon and Quinoa Salad with Lemon-Dill Dressing**

Ingredients:
- 2 salmon fillets
- 1 cup quinoa, rinsed and drained
- 2 cups water or vegetable broth
- 2 cups mixed salad greens
- 1 cucumber, diced
- 1/4 cup red onion, thinly sliced
- 1/4 cup fresh dill, chopped

For Lemon-Dill Dressing:
- Juice of 1 lemon
- 2 tablespoons extra virgin olive oil
- 1 tablespoon Dijon mustard
- 1 teaspoon honey or maple syrup
- Salt and pepper to taste

Instructions:
1. Preheat the oven to 400 °F (200 °C). Arrange the salmon fillets on a baking sheet lined with parchment paper. Season with salt, pepper, and a drizzle of olive oil. Bake for 12-15 minutes, or until the salmon is thoroughly cooked and easily flaked with a fork.
2. Heat water or vegetable broth in a medium saucepan until it boils. Add quinoa, reduce heat to low, cover, and simmer for 15-20 minutes, or until quinoa is cooked and water is absorbed. Fluff with a fork and allow to cool slightly.
3. In a large salad bowl, combine cooked quinoa, mixed salad greens, diced cucumber, thinly sliced red onion, and chopped fresh dill.
4. In a small bowl, whisk together lemon juice, extra virgin olive oil, Dijon mustard, honey or maple syrup, salt, and pepper to make the lemon-dill dressing.
5. Flake the baked salmon into chunks and add to the salad bowl. Drizzle the lemon-dill dressing over the salad and toss gently to coat all the ingredients.

6. Serve the salmon and quinoa salad immediately as a satisfying and nutritious meal. Enjoy!

Nutritional Information (per serving): Calories: 400, Protein: 30g, Fat: 20g, Carbohydrates: 25g, Fiber: 4g, Calcium: 60mg Cooking Time: 30 minutes

5. **Flaxseed Banana Bread**

Ingredients:
- 2 cups whole wheat flour
- 1/2 cup ground flaxseeds
- 1 teaspoon baking powder
- 1/2 teaspoon baking soda
- 1/4 teaspoon salt
- 3 ripe bananas, mashed
- 1/2 cup plain Greek yogurt
- 1/4 cup honey or maple syrup
- 2 eggs
- 1/4 cup unsweetened almond milk
- 1 teaspoon vanilla extract

Instructions:
1. Preheat the oven to 350°F (175°C). Grease a loaf pan with olive oil or line with parchment paper.
2. In a large mixing bowl, combine whole wheat flour, ground flaxseeds, baking powder, baking soda, and salt.
3. In a separate bowl, whisk together mashed bananas, Greek yogurt, honey or maple syrup, eggs, almond milk, and vanilla extract until well combined.
4. Pour the wet ingredients into the dry ingredients and mix just until combined. Take care not to overmix.
5. Pour the batter into the prepared loaf pan and distribute evenly.
6. Bake in the preheated oven for 50-60 minutes, or until a toothpick inserted into the center comes out clean.
7. Remove the banana bread from the oven and let it cool in the pan for 10 minutes before transferring it to a wire rack to cool completely.
8. Slice and serve the flaxseed banana bread as a delicious and nutritious treat. Enjoy!

Nutritional Information (per serving): Calories: 200, Protein: 6g, Fat: 8g, Carbohydrates: 30g, Fiber: 5g, Calcium: 40mg Preparation Time: 15 minutes, Cooking Time: 60 minutes

Chapter 6: Bone-Building Beverages

A. Benefits of bone-boosting drinks

Bone-boosting drinks are beverages specially formulated to support bone health by providing essential nutrients that promote bone strength and density. Here are some key benefits of incorporating bone-boosting drinks into your diet:

1. **Calcium Supplementation**: Many bone-boosting drinks are fortified with calcium, a mineral essential for building and maintaining strong bones. Adequate calcium intake is crucial for bone health, especially during periods of growth, such as childhood and adolescence, and later in life to prevent bone loss.

2. **Vitamin D Absorption**: Some bone-boosting drinks contain vitamin D, which plays a vital role in calcium absorption and bone mineralization. Vitamin D helps regulate calcium levels in the body and ensures that calcium is properly utilized to strengthen bones and teeth.

3. **Magnesium and Phosphorus**: Bone-boosting drinks may also contain magnesium and phosphorus, two minerals that work synergistically with calcium to support bone health. Magnesium is involved in bone formation and regulates calcium levels, while phosphorus helps strengthen bone structure and maintain bone density.

4. **Collagen Support**: Collagen is a protein found in bones, cartilage, and connective tissues, providing strength and flexibility to the skeletal system. Some bone-boosting drinks contain collagen peptides, which may support bone health by promoting collagen synthesis and improving bone density.

5. **Antioxidant Protection**: Certain bone-boosting drinks contain antioxidants such as vitamin C and vitamin E, which help protect bone cells from oxidative damage caused by free radicals. Antioxidants can reduce inflammation and oxidative stress in the body, which are risk factors for bone loss and osteoporosis.

6. **Hydration**: Staying hydrated is essential for overall health, including bone health. Bone-boosting drinks provide hydration along with essential nutrients, helping maintain optimal fluid balance in the body and supporting cellular functions related to bone metabolism.

7. **Convenience and Accessibility**: Bone-boosting drinks are often convenient and accessible options for individuals who may have difficulty meeting their

nutritional needs through diet alone. They can be easily incorporated into daily routines and provide a quick and efficient way to support bone health on the go.

B. Recipes for nutrient-rich beverages

1. Kale and Pineapple Smoothie

Ingredients:

- 2 cups kale leaves, stems removed
- 1 cup frozen pineapple chunks
- 1 banana, peeled
- 1 cup unsweetened almond milk
- 1 tablespoon chia seeds
- 1 tablespoon honey or maple syrup (optional)
- Ice cubes (optional)

Instructions:

1. Place kale leaves, frozen pineapple chunks, banana, unsweetened almond milk, chia seeds, and honey or maple syrup (if using) in a blender.
2. Blend on high speed until smooth and creamy, adding ice cubes if desired for a colder consistency.
3. Pour the kale and pineapple smoothie into glasses and serve immediately for maximum freshness.

Nutritional Information (per serving): Calories: 150, Protein: 4g, Fat: 3g, Carbohydrates: 30g, Fiber: 6g, Calcium: 150mg Preparation Time: 5 minutes

2. Golden Milk Latte with Turmeric and Almond Milk

Ingredients:

- 2 cups unsweetened almond milk
- 1 teaspoon ground turmeric

- 1/2 teaspoon ground cinnamon
- 1/4 teaspoon ground ginger
- 1 tablespoon honey or maple syrup
- 1 teaspoon coconut oil
- Pinch of black pepper (optional, to enhance turmeric absorption)

Instructions:

1. In a small saucepan, heat unsweetened almond milk over medium heat until warm but not boiling.
2. Whisk in ground turmeric, ground cinnamon, ground ginger, honey or maple syrup, coconut oil, and black pepper (if using) until well combined.
3. Continue to heat the golden milk latte mixture for 2-3 minutes, stirring occasionally, until heated through and fragrant.
4. Remove from heat and pour the golden milk latte into mugs.
5. Serve the turmeric golden milk latte warm, optionally garnished with a sprinkle of ground cinnamon on top.

Nutritional Information (per serving): Calories: 120, Protein: 1g, Fat: 4g, Carbohydrates: 20g, Fiber: 2g, Calcium: 300mg Cooking Time: 5 minutes

3. **Green Tea Matcha Smoothie**

Ingredients:

- 1 teaspoon matcha green tea powder
- 1 banana, peeled and frozen
- 1 cup unsweetened almond milk
- 1/2 cup plain Greek yogurt
- 1 tablespoon honey or maple syrup (optional)
- Ice cubes (optional)

Instructions:

1. In a blender, combine matcha green tea powder, frozen banana, unsweetened almond milk, plain Greek yogurt, and honey or maple syrup (if using).
2. Blend on high speed until smooth and creamy, adding ice cubes if desired for a colder consistency.
3. Pour the green tea matcha smoothie into glasses and serve immediately for a refreshing and energizing treat.

Nutritional Information (per serving): Calories: 200, Protein: 8g, Fat: 4g, Carbohydrates: 30g, Fiber: 3g, Calcium: 250mg Preparation Time: 5 minutes

4. **Berry Blast Smoothie**

Ingredients:

- 1 cup mixed berries (strawberries, blueberries, raspberries)
- 1/2 banana, peeled
- 1/2 cup spinach leaves
- 1 cup unsweetened coconut water
- 1 tablespoon flaxseeds
- 1 tablespoon honey or maple syrup (optional)
- Ice cubes (optional)

Instructions:

1. In a blender, combine mixed berries, bananas, spinach leaves, unsweetened coconut water, flaxseeds, and honey or maple syrup (if using).
2. Blend on high speed until smooth and creamy, adding ice cubes if desired for a colder consistency.
3. Pour the berry blast smoothie into glasses and serve immediately for a refreshing and antioxidant-rich beverage.

Nutritional Information (per serving): Calories: 150, Protein: 3g, Fat: 3g, Carbohydrates: 30g, Fiber: 7g, Calcium: 80mg Preparation Time: 5 minutes

5. Almond Butter Banana Shake

Ingredients:

- 1 ripe banana, peeled and frozen
- 2 tablespoons almond butter
- 1 cup unsweetened almond milk
- 1 tablespoon honey or maple syrup (optional)
- 1/2 teaspoon vanilla extract
- Pinch of cinnamon (optional)
- Ice cubes (optional)

Instructions:

1. In a blender, combine frozen banana, almond butter, unsweetened almond milk, honey or maple syrup (if using), vanilla extract, and cinnamon (if using).
2. Blend on high speed until smooth and creamy, adding ice cubes if desired for a colder consistency.
3. Pour the almond butter banana shake into glasses and serve immediately for a creamy and satisfying treat.

Nutritional Information (per serving): Calories: 250, Protein: 6g, Fat: 12g, Carbohydrates: 30g, Fiber: 5g, Calcium: 200mg Preparation Time: 5 minutes

6. Spinach and Pineapple Green Smoothie

Ingredients:

- 2 cups fresh spinach leaves
- 1 cup frozen pineapple chunks
- 1/2 banana, peeled
- 1 tablespoon chia seeds
- 1 cup unsweetened coconut water

- Juice of 1/2 lime
- Ice cubes (optional)

Instructions:

1. In a blender, combine fresh spinach leaves, frozen pineapple chunks, banana, chia seeds, unsweetened coconut water, and lime juice.

2. Blend on high speed until smooth and creamy, adding ice cubes if desired for a colder consistency.

3. Pour the spinach and pineapple green smoothie into glasses and serve immediately for a refreshing and nutrient-packed beverage.

Nutritional Information (per serving): Calories: 120, Protein: 4g, Fat: 3g, Carbohydrates: 25g, Fiber: 6g, Calcium: 120mg Preparation Time: 5 minutes

Chapter 7: Meal Planning for Bone Health

A. Tips for creating balanced meals

Creating balanced meals is essential for meeting your nutritional needs, supporting overall health, and maintaining energy levels throughout the day. Here are some tips to help you create well-balanced meals:

1. **Incorporate a Variety of Food Groups**: Aim to include foods from all major food groups in your meals, including fruits, vegetables, whole grains, lean proteins, and healthy fats. Each food group provides different nutrients that are essential for optimal health.
2. **Fill Half Your Plate with Fruits and Vegetables**: Make fruits and vegetables the focal point of your meals by filling at least half of your plate with colorful produce. Choose a variety of fruits and vegetables to ensure you're getting a wide range of vitamins, minerals, and antioxidants.
3. **Choose Whole Grains**: Opt for whole grains such as brown rice, quinoa, barley, oats, whole wheat bread, pasta, and couscous. Whole grains are rich in fiber, vitamins, and minerals, and they provide sustained energy to keep you feeling full and satisfied.
4. **Include Lean Proteins**: Incorporate lean sources of protein into your meals, such as poultry, fish, tofu, tempeh, beans, lentils, and legumes. Protein is essential for building and repairing tissues, supporting muscle growth, and maintaining satiety.
5. **Add Healthy Fats**: Include sources of healthy fats in your meals, such as avocados, nuts, seeds, olive oil, and fatty fish like salmon and mackerel. Healthy fats promote brain health, hormone production, and nutrient absorption.
6. **Watch Portion Sizes**: Be mindful of portion sizes to avoid overeating and ensure you're consuming the right amount of calories for your body's needs. Use smaller plates and bowls, and pay attention to hunger and fullness cues to prevent overindulgence.
7. **Limit Added Sugars and Processed Foods**: Minimize your intake of added sugars, refined carbohydrates, and processed foods, which can contribute to weight gain, inflammation, and chronic diseases. Instead, focus on whole, unprocessed foods that are nutrient-dense and provide sustained energy.

8. **Stay Hydrated**: Drink plenty of water throughout the day to stay hydrated and support optimal bodily functions. Water is essential for digestion, nutrient absorption, metabolism, and maintaining electrolyte balance.
9. **Plan Ahead**: Take the time to plan your meals and snacks ahead of time to ensure you have nutritious options available when hunger strikes. Meal prepping and batch cooking can save time and make healthy eating more convenient.
10. **Listen to Your Body**: Pay attention to how different foods make you feel and adjust your meals accordingly. Eat when you're hungry and stop when you're satisfied, practicing mindful eating to savor each bite and appreciate the flavors and textures of your food.

B. Sample meal plans

Day	Breakfast	Lunch	Dinner
Day 1	Scrambled eggs with spinach and tomatoes	Grilled chicken salad with avocado	Baked salmon with quinoa and roasted vegetables
Day 2	Greek yogurt with berries and granola	Turkey and vegetable wrap with hummus	Stir-fried tofu with broccoli and brown rice
Day 3	Oatmeal with sliced bananas and almonds	Quinoa salad with chickpeas and feta cheese	Lentil soup with whole wheat bread
Day 4	Whole wheat toast with almond butter	Grilled vegetable and feta cheese sandwich	Spaghetti with marinara sauce and side salad
Day 5	Smoothie with spinach, banana, and almond milk	Black bean and corn salad with avocado	Grilled shrimp with quinoa and steamed asparagus
Day 6	Cottage cheese with pineapple chunks	Lentil and vegetable curry with brown rice	Baked chicken breast with sweet potato mash
Day 7	Avocado toast with poached egg	Tuna salad with mixed greens and whole-grain crackers	Vegetable stir-fry with tofu and jasmine rice

Day 8	Whole grain pancakes with fresh berries	Chicken and vegetable stir-fry with rice noodles	Grilled salmon with roasted Brussels sprouts
Day 9	Smoothie bowl with mixed berries and granola	Spinach and feta stuffed chicken breast	Quinoa and black bean stuffed peppers
Day 10	Breakfast burrito with scrambled eggs, black beans, and salsa	Turkey and avocado wrap with mixed greens	Baked cod with lemon-dill sauce and steamed broccoli
Day 11	Yogurt parfait with granola and sliced peaches	Veggie burger with sweet potato fries	Vegetable curry with coconut milk and brown rice
Day 12	Whole grain waffles with strawberries and Greek yogurt	Mediterranean quinoa salad with olives and feta	Grilled tofu with teriyaki sauce and mixed vegetables
Day 13	Egg muffins with spinach, tomatoes, and feta cheese	Caprese salad with basil pesto dressing	Whole wheat pasta primavera with a side salad
Day 14	Chia seed pudding with mixed berries	Chicken Caesar salad with whole wheat croutons	Lentil soup with crusty whole-grain bread
Day 15	Banana smoothie with almond milk and peanut butter	Grilled vegetable and hummus wrap	Baked sweet potatoes with black bean salsa
Day 16	Breakfast quesadilla with eggs, cheese, and salsa	Quinoa and black bean salad with avocado	Salmon teriyaki with stir-fried vegetables and brown rice
Day 17	Overnight oats with almond milk, chia seeds, and berries	Turkey and avocado wrap with mixed greens	Vegetable curry with tofu and quinoa
Day 18	Whole grain toast with mashed avocado and sliced tomatoes	Chickpea and vegetable stir-fry with brown rice	Grilled chicken breast with roasted vegetables

Day 19	Smoothie with kale, pineapple, and coconut water	Greek salad with grilled chicken	Baked cod with Mediterranean couscous and steamed asparagus
Day 20	Breakfast burrito bowl with scrambled eggs, black beans, and salsa	Lentil and vegetable soup with whole-grain bread	Stuffed bell peppers with quinoa and black beans
Day 21	Yogurt parfait with granola and mixed berries	Tuna and white bean salad with lemon vinaigrette	Teriyaki tofu with broccoli and brown rice

C. Suggestions for breakfast, lunch, dinner, and snacks

Breakfast:

1. **Greek Yogurt Parfait with Granola and Mixed Berries:**

Ingredients:
- 1 cup Greek yogurt
- 1/2 cup granola
- 1/2 cup of mixed berries (such as strawberries, blueberries, and raspberries)
- Honey or maple syrup (optional, for sweetness)

Instructions:
1. In a glass or bowl, combine the Greek yogurt, granola, and mixed berries.
2. Repeat the layers until all ingredients are used, ending with a layer of mixed berries on top.
3. Drizzle honey or maple syrup on top if desired for added sweetness.
4. Serve immediately and enjoy!

Nutritional Information (per serving): Calories: 300, Protein: 20g, Fat: 10g, Carbohydrates: 35g, Fiber: 5g Preparation Time: 5 minutes

2. **Scrambled Eggs with Spinach and Tomatoes on Whole Wheat Toast:**

Ingredients:
- 2 eggs
- Handful of spinach leaves
- 1 tomato, diced
- 2 slices of whole wheat toast
- Salt and pepper to taste

- Olive oil or cooking spray

Instructions:
1. In a bowl, whisk the eggs with salt and pepper.
2. Heat olive oil or cooking spray in a non-stick skillet over medium heat.
3. Add spinach leaves and diced tomatoes to the skillet and sauté until spinach is wilted and tomatoes are softened.
4. Pour the whisked eggs into the skillet and cook, stirring occasionally, until the eggs are scrambled and fully cooked.
5. Toast the whole wheat bread slices until they're golden brown.
6. Serve the scrambled eggs with spinach and tomatoes on top of the whole wheat toast.
7. Add additional salt and pepper if desired.
8. Enjoy your nutritious breakfast!

Nutritional Information (per serving): Calories: 250, Protein: 15g, Fat: 10g, Carbohydrates: 25g, Fiber: 5g Cooking Time: 10 minutes

3. **Overnight Oats with Almond Milk, Chia Seeds, and Sliced Bananas:**

Ingredients:
- 1/2 cup rolled oats
- 1 cup unsweetened almond milk
- 1 tablespoon chia seeds
- 1 ripe banana, sliced
- Honey or maple syrup (optional, for sweetness)

Instructions:
1. In a bowl or jar, combine rolled oats, almond milk, and chia seeds.
2. Stir well to combine, then cover and refrigerate overnight.
3. In the morning, stir the overnight oats mixture and top with sliced bananas.
4. Drizzle honey or maple syrup on top if desired for added sweetness.
5. Serve chilled and enjoy a nutritious and filling breakfast!

Nutritional Information (per serving): Calories: 300, Protein: 7g, Fat: 8g, Carbohydrates: 50g, Fiber: 10g Preparation Time: 5 minutes

4. **Smoothie Bowl with Spinach, Banana, and Almond Butter Topped with Nuts and Seeds:**

Ingredients:
- 1 cup spinach leaves
- 1 ripe banana
- 1 tablespoon almond butter
- 1/2 cup unsweetened almond milk
- 1 tablespoon nuts and seeds of your choice (such as almonds, walnuts, chia seeds, or hemp seeds)
- Optional toppings: sliced fresh fruit, granola, coconut flakes

Instructions:
1. In a blender, combine spinach leaves, banana, almond butter, and unsweetened almond milk.
2. Blend until smooth and creamy, adding more almond milk as needed to achieve the desired consistency.
3. Pour the smoothie into a bowl.
4. Top with nuts and seeds of your choice, along with any optional toppings you like.
5. Serve immediately and enjoy a refreshing and nutritious smoothie bowl!

Nutritional Information (per serving): Calories: 300, Protein: 8g, Fat: 15g, Carbohydrates: 35g, Fiber: 8g Preparation Time: 5 minutes

5. **Whole Grain Pancakes with Fresh Fruit and a Dollop of Greek Yogurt:**

Ingredients:
- 1 cup whole-grain pancake mix
- 3/4 cup water or milk of your choice
- Fresh fruit of your choice (such as berries, sliced bananas, or peaches)
- Greek yogurt
- Maple syrup or honey (optional, for serving)

Instructions:
1. In a mixing bowl, combine whole-grain pancake mix and water or milk according to package instructions.
2. Stir until smooth, but do not overmix.
3. Heat a nonstick skillet or griddle over medium heat and lightly coat with cooking spray or butter.

4. Pour the pancake batter onto the skillet, using about 1/4 cup of batter for each pancake.
5. Cook until bubbles appear on top of the pancakes, then flip and cook until golden brown on both sides.
6. Repeat with the remaining batter.
7. Serve the pancakes topped with fresh fruit, a dollop of Greek yogurt, and a drizzle of maple syrup or honey if desired.
8. Enjoy your wholesome and delicious breakfast!

Nutritional Information (per serving): Calories: 250, Protein: 10g, Fat: 5g, Carbohydrates: 45g, Fiber: 7g Cooking Time: 15 minutes

These recipes provide nutritious and delicious options for breakfast, ensuring a well-balanced start to your day. Adjust ingredients and portion sizes based on individual preferences and dietary needs. Enjoy!

Lunch:

1. **Grilled Chicken Salad with Mixed Greens, Cherry Tomatoes, Cucumber, and Balsamic Vinaigrette:**

Ingredients:
- 2 boneless, skinless chicken breasts
- 4 cups mixed salad greens
- 1 cup cherry tomatoes, halved
- 1 cucumber, sliced
- Balsamic vinaigrette dressing
- Salt and pepper to taste
- Olive oil for grilling

Instructions:
1. Preheat the grill or grill pan to medium-high heat.
2. Season the chicken breasts with salt, pepper, and a drizzle of olive oil.
3. Grill the chicken breasts for 6-8 minutes per side, or until cooked through and no longer pink in the center.
4. Remove the chicken from the grill and let it rest for a few minutes before slicing it thinly.
5. In a large bowl, toss the mixed salad greens, cherry tomatoes, and cucumber with balsamic vinaigrette dressing.

6. Divide the salad mixture among plates and top with sliced grilled chicken.
7. Serve immediately and enjoy your tasty and nutritious grilled chicken salad!

Nutritional Information (per serving): Calories: 300, Protein: 30g, Fat: 10g, Carbohydrates: 20g, Fiber: 5g Cooking Time: 15 minutes

2. **Quinoa and Black Bean Salad with Avocado, Corn, Bell Peppers, and Lime-Cilantro Dressing:**

Ingredients:
- 1 cup of quinoa, cooked according to package directions
- 1 can black beans, rinsed and drained
- 1 avocado, diced
- 1 cup corn kernels (fresh, canned, or frozen)
- 1 bell pepper, diced (any color)
- Lime-cilantro dressing (mix lime juice, olive oil, minced garlic, chopped cilantro, salt, and pepper)
- Salt and pepper to taste

Instructions:
1. In a large bowl, combine cooked quinoa, black beans, diced avocado, corn kernels, and diced bell pepper.
2. Drizzle the lime-cilantro dressing over the salad and toss gently to coat.
3. Add salt and pepper to taste.
4. Serve immediately or refrigerate until ready to serve.
5. Enjoy this refreshing and flavorful quinoa and black bean salad as a nutritious meal or side dish!

Nutritional Information (per serving): Calories: 350, Protein: 10g, Fat: 15g, Carbohydrates: 45g, Fiber: 10g Preparation Time: 20 minutes

3. **Turkey and Avocado Wrap with Whole Grain Tortilla, Lettuce, Tomato, and Mustard:**

Ingredients:
- 2 whole grain tortillas
- 1/2 lb sliced turkey breast
- 1 avocado, sliced
- Lettuce leaves
- Tomato slices

- Mustard

Instructions:
1. Lay out the whole-grain tortillas on a clean surface.
2. Spread mustard evenly over each tortilla.
3. Layer sliced turkey breast, avocado slices, lettuce leaves, and tomato slices on top of the tortillas.
4. Roll up the tortillas tightly to form wraps.
5. Cut the wraps in half diagonally and serve immediately, or wrap them in foil for later.
6. Enjoy this delicious and nutritious turkey and avocado wrap for a satisfying meal on the go!

Nutritional Information (per serving): Calories: 400, Protein: 25g, Fat: 15g, Carbohydrates: 40g, Fiber: 8g Preparation Time: 10 minutes

4. Lentil Soup with Crusty Whole Grain Bread and a Side of Mixed Greens:

Ingredients:
- 1 cup dried lentils, rinsed and drained
- 4 cups vegetable broth
- 1 onion, chopped
- 2 carrots, diced
- 2 celery stalks, diced
- 2 cloves garlic, minced
- 1 teaspoon dried thyme
- Salt and pepper to taste
- Crusty whole grain bread for serving
- Mixed greens for a side salad

Instructions:
1. In a large pot, combine lentils, vegetable broth, chopped onion, diced carrots, diced celery, minced garlic, and dried thyme.
2. Bring the soup to a boil on high heat, then reduce to a low heat and simmer for 20-25 minutes, or until the lentils and vegetables are soft.
3. Season the soup with salt and pepper as desired.
4. Serve the lentil soup hot with crusty whole-grain bread for dipping.
5. Enjoy a side salad of mixed greens dressed with your favorite vinaigrette.

Nutritional Information (per serving): Calories: 300, Protein: 15g, Fat: 5g, Carbohydrates: 50g, Fiber: 15g Cooking Time: 30 minutes

5. **Veggie Burger on a Whole Wheat Bun with Sweet Potato Fries and a Side Salad:**

Ingredients:
- Two vegetable burger patties (store-bought or homemade)
- 2 whole wheat burger buns.
- 1 big sweet potato, cut into fries.
- 1 tablespoon olive oil
- Salt and pepper to taste
- Mixed greens for a side salad
- Your favorite salad dressing

Instructions:
1. Preheat the oven to 425°F (220°C).
2. Place the sweet potato fries on a baking sheet, drizzle with olive oil, and season with salt and pepper.
3. Toss the sweet potato fries to coat evenly in the oil and seasoning.
4. Bake the sweet potato fries in the preheated oven for 20-25 minutes, or until golden and crispy.
5. While the sweet potato fries are baking, cook the veggie burger patties according to package instructions or prepare homemade veggie burgers on a skillet or grill.
6. Toast the whole wheat burger buns if desired.
7. Assemble the veggie burgers on the whole wheat buns and serve with a side of sweet potato fries and mixed greens dressed with your favorite salad dressing.
8. Enjoy this hearty and satisfying veggie burger meal!

Nutritional Information (per serving): Calories: 400, Protein: 20g, Fat: 10g, Carbohydrates: 60g, Fiber: 12g Cooking Time: 30 minutes

These recipes offer nutritious and delicious meal options that are easy to prepare and enjoy. Adjust ingredients and portion sizes based on individual preferences and dietary needs. Enjoy your homemade meals!

Dinner:

1. Baked Salmon with Quinoa Pilaf and Steamed Broccoli:

Ingredients:
- 2 salmon fillets
- 1 cup quinoa, rinsed and drained
- 2 cups vegetable or chicken broth
- 2 cups broccoli florets
- Olive oil
- Salt and pepper to taste
- Lemon wedges for serving

Instructions:
1. Preheat the oven to 375°F (190°C).
2. Season the salmon fillets with salt, pepper, and a drizzle of olive oil.
3. Arrange the seasoned salmon fillets on a baking sheet lined with parchment paper.
4. In a saucepan, bring the vegetable or chicken broth to a boil, then add the rinsed quinoa.
5. Reduce the heat to low, cover, and simmer for 15-20 minutes, or until the quinoa is cooked and the liquid is absorbed.
6. While the quinoa is cooking, steam the broccoli florets until tender.
7. Bake the salmon fillets in the preheated oven for 12-15 minutes, or until cooked through and flaky.
8. Serve the baked salmon with quinoa pilaf and steamed broccoli.
9. Garnish with lemon wedges and enjoy your delicious and nutritious meal!

Nutritional Information (per serving): Calories: 400, Protein: 30g, Fat: 15g, Carbohydrates: 35g, Fiber: 5g Cooking Time: 25 minutes

2. Stir-fried tofu with Mixed Vegetables and Brown Rice:

Ingredients:
- 1 block of firm tofu, drained and cubed
- 2 cups mixed veggies (such as bell peppers, broccoli, carrots, and snow peas)
- 2 cups cooked brown rice
- 2 tablespoons soy sauce
- 1 tablespoon sesame oil

- 2 cloves garlic, minced
- Salt and pepper to taste
- Green onions for garnish (optional)

Instructions:
1. Heat sesame oil in a large skillet or wok over medium-high heat.
2. Add minced garlic to the skillet and sauté for 1-2 minutes, or until fragrant.
3. Add cubed tofu to the skillet and cook until golden brown on all sides.
4. Stir-fry the mixed vegetables in the skillet until they are crisp and tender.
5. Stir in cooked brown rice, soy sauce, salt, and pepper, and cook for another 2-3 minutes.
6. Remove from heat and garnish with chopped green onions if desired.
7. Serve hot and enjoy this flavorful and nutritious stir-fry!

Nutritional Information (per serving): Calories: 350, Protein: 20g, Fat: 10g, Carbohydrates: 45g, Fiber: 8g Cooking Time: 20 minutes

3. **Spaghetti with Marinara Sauce, Lean Ground Turkey, and a Side of Roasted Vegetables:**

Ingredients:
- 8 oz whole wheat spaghetti
- 1 lb lean ground turkey
- 2 cups marinara sauce (store-bought or homemade)
- 2 cups mixed vegetables (such as zucchini, bell peppers, and onions), chopped
- Olive oil
- Salt and pepper to taste
- Grated Parmesan cheese for serving (optional)

Instructions:
1. Preheat the oven to 400°F (200°C).
2. Cook whole wheat spaghetti according to package instructions until al dente.
3. In a large skillet, heat olive oil over medium heat and cook lean ground turkey until no longer pink.
4. Add marinara sauce to the skillet with cooked ground turkey and simmer for 5-10 minutes.
5. Meanwhile, spread chopped mixed vegetables on a baking sheet, drizzle with olive oil and season with salt and pepper.

6. Roast the vegetables in the preheated oven for 15-20 minutes, or until tender and lightly browned.
7. Serve spaghetti topped with marinara sauce and lean ground turkey, alongside a side of roasted vegetables.
8. Garnish with grated Parmesan cheese if desired.
9. Enjoy this comforting and nutritious pasta dish!

Nutritional Information (per serving): Calories: 400, Protein: 25g, Fat: 10g, Carbohydrates: 50g, Fiber: 8g Cooking Time: 30 minutes

4. **Grilled Shrimp Skewers with Pineapple Salsa and Wild Rice:**

Ingredients:
- 1 pound of large shrimp, peeled and deveined.
- 1 cup diced pineapple
- 1/2 red onion, finely chopped
- 1/4 cup chopped cilantro
- Juice of 1 lime
- Salt and pepper to taste
- 2 cups cooked wild rice
- Skewers (if using wooden skewers, soak in water for 30 minutes before grilling) Skewers (if using wooden skewers, soak in water for 30 minutes before grilling)

Instructions:
1. Preheat the grill to medium-high heat.
2. In a bowl, combine diced pineapple, chopped red onion, chopped cilantro, lime juice, salt, and pepper to make the pineapple salsa.
3. Thread shrimp onto skewers, leaving a little space between each shrimp.
4. Grill the shrimp skewers for 2-3 minutes per side, or until shrimp are pink and opaque.
5. Serve grilled shrimp skewers with pineapple salsa and cooked wild rice.
6. Enjoy this delicious and nutritious seafood dish!

Nutritional Information (per serving): Calories: 300, Protein: 25g, Fat: 5g, Carbohydrates: 35g, Fiber: 3g Cooking Time: 15 minutes

5. **Vegetable Curry with Coconut Milk, Chickpeas, and Cauliflower served over Basmati Rice:**

Ingredients:
- 1 tablespoon coconut oil
- 1 onion, diced
- 2 cloves garlic, minced
- 1 tablespoon grated ginger
- 2 teaspoons curry powder
- 1 teaspoon ground cumin
- 1/2 teaspoon ground turmeric
- 1 can (14 oz) coconut milk
- 1 can (14 oz) chickpeas, rinsed and drained
- 1 small head of cauliflower, cut into florets
- Salt and pepper to taste
- Cooked basmati rice for serving

Instructions:
1. Heat coconut oil in a large skillet or pot over medium heat.
2. Add diced onion, minced garlic, and grated ginger to the skillet and cook until softened and fragrant.
3. Stir in curry powder, ground cumin, and ground turmeric, and cook for another minute.
4. Pour in coconut milk and bring the mixture to a simmer.
5. Add chickpeas and cauliflower florets to the skillet and stir to combine.
6. Cover and simmer for 15-20 minutes, or until the cauliflower is tender.
7. Season with salt and pepper to taste.
8. Serve vegetable curry over cooked basmati rice.
9. Enjoy this aromatic and flavorful curry as a satisfying vegetarian meal!

Nutritional Information (per serving): Calories: 400, Protein: 10g, Fat: 20g, Carbohydrates: 45g, Fiber: 8g Cooking Time: 30 minutes

Snacks:
1. **Apple Slices with Almond Butter:**

Ingredients:
- 1 apple, sliced

- 2 tablespoons almond butter

Instructions:
1. Wash and slice the apple into wedges or rounds.
2. Spread almond butter on each apple slice.
3. Arrange the apple slices on a plate and serve immediately.

Nutritional Information (per serving): Calories: 150, Protein: 3g, Fat: 8g, Carbohydrates: 18g, Fiber: 5g Preparation Time: 5 minutes

2. **Carrot Sticks and Hummus:**

Ingredients:
- 2 carrots, peeled and cut into sticks
- 1/4 cup hummus

Instructions:
1. Wash and peel the carrots, then cut them into sticks.
2. Serve the carrot sticks with hummus for dipping.

Nutritional Information (per serving): Calories: 100, Protein: 3g, Fat: 5g, Carbohydrates: 12g, Fiber: 4g Preparation Time: 5 minutes

3. **Mixed Nuts and Dried Fruits:**

Ingredients:
- 1/4 cup mixed nuts (such as almonds, walnuts, and cashews)
- 1/4 cup mixed dried fruits (such as raisins, apricots, and cranberries)

Instructions:
1. Measure out the mixed nuts and dried fruits.
2. Combine them in a bowl or portion them out into individual servings.

Nutritional Information (per serving): Calories: 200, Protein: 5g, Fat: 12g, Carbohydrates: 20g, Fiber: 4g Preparation Time: 2 minutes

4. **Cottage Cheese with Pineapple Chunks:**

Ingredients:
- 1/2 cup cottage cheese
- 1/2 cup pineapple chunks (fresh or canned in juice)

Instructions:
1. Spoon the cottage cheese into a bowl.
2. Top with pineapple chunks and serve immediately.

Nutritional Information (per serving): Calories: 150, Protein: 14g, Fat: 2g, Carbohydrates: 20g, Fiber: 2g Preparation Time: 2 minutes

5. **Whole Grain Crackers with Sliced Cheese and Grapes:**

Ingredients:
- 6 whole grain crackers
- 2 slices of cheese (such as cheddar or Swiss), cut into squares
- 1/2 cup grapes, washed

Instructions:
1. Arrange the whole grain crackers on a plate or serving board.
2. Top each cracker with a slice of cheese.
3. Serve alongside grapes for a balanced snack.

Nutritional Information (per serving): Calories: 200, Protein: 10g, Fat: 8g, Carbohydrates: 25g, Fiber: 4g Preparation Time: 5 minutes

Chapter 8: Beyond the Plate: Lifestyle Tips for Strong Bones

A. Additional lifestyle factors for bone health

In addition to nutrition, several lifestyle factors play a crucial role in maintaining strong and healthy bones. Consider incorporating the following practices into your daily routine to support optimal bone health:

1. Regular Exercise: Engage in weight-bearing and resistance exercises such as walking, jogging, dancing, weightlifting, and yoga. These activities help stimulate bone growth and increase bone density.
2. Adequate Sun Exposure: Spend time outdoors to allow your skin to produce vitamin D, which is essential for calcium absorption and bone health. Aim for at least 15-30 minutes of sun exposure on your arms, legs, or face several times a week, especially during the midday sun.
3. Quit Smoking: Smoking can weaken bones and increase the risk of fractures. If you smoke, consider quitting or seeking support to help you quit smoking for the benefit of your bone health and overall well-being.
4. Limit Alcohol Intake: Excessive alcohol consumption can interfere with calcium absorption and reduce bone density. Limit alcohol intake to moderate levels, which is generally defined as up to one drink per day for women and up to two drinks per day for men.
5. Maintain a Healthy Body Weight: Being underweight or overweight can negatively impact bone health. Aim to maintain a healthy body weight through a balanced diet and regular exercise to reduce the risk of bone-related problems.
6. Stay Hydrated: Drink an adequate amount of water daily to support overall health, including bone health. Water is essential for transporting nutrients to cells and removing waste products from the body, which contributes to bone strength and integrity.
7. Get Sufficient Sleep: Adequate sleep is crucial for bone remodeling and repair. Aim for 7-9 hours of quality sleep each night to support optimal bone health and overall well-being.
8. Manage Stress: Chronic stress can affect hormone levels and bone health. Practice stress-reducing techniques such as deep breathing, meditation, yoga, or spending time in nature to promote relaxation and support bone health.

B. Practical tips for maintaining strong bones

1. Consume a Balanced Diet: Include a variety of nutrient-rich foods in your diet, focusing on calcium-rich foods like dairy products, leafy greens, and fortified foods, as well as vitamin D sources like fatty fish, eggs, and fortified foods. Also, prioritize foods rich in magnesium, phosphorus, and vitamin K, which are essential for bone health.
2. Engage in Weight-Bearing Exercises: Incorporate weight-bearing and resistance exercises into your routine, such as walking, jogging, dancing, strength training, and yoga. These activities help build and maintain bone density, promoting stronger bones.
3. Ensure Adequate Vitamin D Intake: Get sufficient vitamin D through sun exposure, dietary sources, or supplements if necessary. Aim for 15-30 minutes of sunlight on your skin a few times per week and include vitamin D-rich foods like fatty fish, fortified dairy products, and egg yolks in your diet.
4. Limit Alcohol and Caffeine Intake: Excessive alcohol and caffeine consumption can interfere with calcium absorption and contribute to bone loss. Limit alcohol intake to moderate levels and consume caffeine in moderation.
5. Avoid Smoking and Tobacco Products: Smoking can weaken bones and increase the risk of fractures. If you smoke, consider quitting to protect your bone health and overall well-being.
6. Practice Good Posture and Body Mechanics: Maintain proper posture and body mechanics to reduce the risk of bone and joint problems. Use ergonomically designed furniture and equipment and practice safe lifting techniques to protect your spine and bones.
7. Prevent Falls: Take steps to prevent falls by removing tripping hazards from your home, installing handrails and grab bars, wearing supportive footwear, and using assistive devices if necessary. Regular exercise can also improve balance and coordination, reducing the risk of falls and fractures.
8. Stay Hydrated: Drink plenty of water throughout the day to support overall health, including bone health. Adequate hydration helps maintain proper mineral balance and bone density.

9. Get Regular Bone Density Screenings: Discuss with your healthcare provider whether you need bone density screenings, especially if you have risk factors for osteoporosis or low bone density. Early detection and intervention can help to avoid fractures and complications.
10. Consult with a Healthcare Professional: If you have concerns about your bone health or are at risk for osteoporosis, seek guidance from a healthcare professional. They can provide personalized recommendations and interventions to support your bone health and reduce the risk of fractures.

C. *Strategies for incorporating healthy habits into daily life*

1. Set Realistic Goals: Start by setting achievable goals that align with your lifestyle and priorities. Break down larger goals into smaller, more manageable steps to make them more achievable.
2. Plan Ahead: Take time to plan your meals, exercise routine, and daily activities in advance. Schedule time for physical activity, meal preparation, and relaxation to ensure you prioritize your health amidst your busy schedule.
3. Create a Routine: Establish a consistent daily routine that includes healthy habits such as regular exercise, balanced meals, adequate sleep, and stress management techniques. Consistency is essential for forming lasting habits.
4. Make Healthy Choices Convenient: Keep healthy snacks, such as fruits, nuts, and yogurt, readily available at home and work. Stock your kitchen with nutritious ingredients for quick and easy meal preparation. Choose exercise activities that you enjoy and can easily incorporate into your daily routine.
5. Practice Mindful Eating: Pay attention to your hunger and fullness cues, and eat slowly to savor and enjoy your meals. Avoid distractions such as electronic devices while eating to focus on the sensory experience of eating and promote mindful eating habits.
6. Stay Active Throughout the Day: Find opportunities to incorporate physical activity into your daily routine, such as taking the stairs instead of the elevator, walking or biking to work, or scheduling short activity breaks throughout the day. Aim for at least 30 minutes of moderate-intensity exercise on most days of the week.

7. Seek Social Support: Surround yourself with supportive friends, family members, or coworkers who share your health goals or encourage healthy behaviors. Joining fitness classes, sports teams, or community groups can also provide social support and accountability.
8. Practice Self-Care: Prioritize self-care activities that promote physical, mental, and emotional well-being, such as meditation, yoga, relaxation techniques, hobbies, or spending time outdoors. Taking care of yourself allows you to better cope with stress and maintain a healthy lifestyle.
9. Monitor Your Progress: Keep track of your progress toward your health goals using tools such as a journal, mobile apps, or wearable fitness trackers. Celebrate your achievements and milestones along the way to stay motivated and focused on your journey to better health.
10. Be Flexible and Adapt: Recognize that life can be unpredictable, and be willing to adapt your plans and goals as needed. Be kind to yourself if you experience setbacks or challenges, and focus on making progress rather than perfection.

D. Sample exercises for stronger bone

1. Weight-Bearing Exercises:
   - Walking: Take brisk walks outdoors or on a treadmill to stimulate bone growth and maintain bone density.
   - Jogging or Running: Include jogging or running in your exercise routine to provide impact and stress on your bones, thereby increasing bone strength.
   - Stair Climbing: Use stairs for a cardiovascular workout that also strengthens bones in your legs, hips, and spine.
2. Strength Training:
   - Squats: Perform bodyweight squats or use weights to strengthen the muscles around your hips, thighs, and buttocks, which also helps build bone density in these areas.
   - Lunges: Incorporate forward, backward, or side lunges to strengthen leg muscles and improve bone density in the lower body.

- Deadlifts: Use proper form to perform deadlifts with weights to target multiple muscle groups, including those in the back, legs, and core, while also promoting bone health.
- Chest Press: Use dumbbells or resistance bands to perform chest presses, which strengthen the muscles in your chest and shoulders while also benefiting bone health.

3. Resistance Training:
   - Resistance Bands: Use resistance bands to perform various exercises, such as bicep curls, tricep extensions, shoulder presses, and rows, to strengthen muscles and bones throughout the body.
   - Bodyweight Exercises: Incorporate bodyweight exercises like push-ups, planks, and wall sits to build strength and stability while also improving bone health.

4. Balance and Stability Exercises:
   - Single-Leg Balance: Stand on one leg while maintaining balance and stability, then switch to the other leg. This exercise helps improve balance and proprioception, reducing the risk of falls and fractures.
   - Tai Chi, a gentle martial art that emphasizes slow, flowing movements and deep breathing, can help you improve your balance, coordination, and bone health.
   - Yoga: Participate in yoga classes or practice yoga poses at home to improve flexibility, strength, and balance while also benefiting bone health.

5. Flexibility and Mobility Exercises:
   - Stretching: Incorporate stretching exercises into your routine to improve flexibility and range of motion, reducing the risk of injury and supporting overall bone health.
   - Pilates: Take Pilates classes or perform Pilates exercises to strengthen muscles, improve posture, and enhance flexibility, which also contributes to better bone health.

6. Functional Exercises:
   - Functional Movements: Perform functional exercises that mimic activities of daily living, such as lifting, bending, reaching, and twisting, to improve strength, mobility, and bone health in a practical context.

Conclusion

A. Recap of key points

1. Understanding Osteoporosis:
   - Osteoporosis is a condition characterized by weakened bones, increasing the risk of fractures.
   - It is essential to prevent osteoporosis through lifestyle choices, including diet, exercise, and other healthy habits.
2. Importance of Preventing Osteoporosis:
   - Preventing osteoporosis is crucial for maintaining strong and healthy bones throughout life.
   - Healthy bones support mobility, independence, and overall well-being, reducing the risk of fractures and related complications.
3. Role of Nutrition in Bone Health:
   - Nutrition plays a vital role in bone health, with calcium, vitamin D, protein, magnesium, phosphorus, and other nutrients essential for maintaining strong bones.
   - Consuming a balanced diet rich in calcium-rich foods, protein, fruits, vegetables, whole grains, and healthy fats supports optimal bone health.
4. Practical Tips for Maintaining Strong Bones:
   - Engage in weight-bearing exercises, strength training, and balance exercises to promote bone strength and density.
   - Ensure adequate intake of calcium, vitamin D, and other essential nutrients through diet, supplements, or sun exposure.
   - Limit alcohol and caffeine consumption, avoid smoking, and maintain a healthy body weight to support bone health.
5. Incorporating Healthy Habits into Daily Life:
   - Set realistic goals, plan, and create a routine that includes regular exercise, balanced meals, and self-care activities.
   - Make healthy choices convenient, seek social support, and monitor your progress to stay motivated and focused on your health goals.
6. Sample Exercises for Stronger Bones:

- Incorporate weight-bearing exercises, strength training, resistance training, balance and stability exercises, flexibility and mobility exercises, and functional movements into your exercise routine.
- Consult with a healthcare professional or fitness expert before starting a new exercise program, especially if you have existing health concerns or medical conditions.

B. Encouragement for readers to prioritize bone health

Dear Readers,

Your bone health is essential for maintaining mobility, independence, and overall well-being throughout your life. By prioritizing bone health, you can reduce the risk of osteoporosis, fractures, and related complications, allowing you to live life to the fullest.

Remember that prevention is key when it comes to osteoporosis. By adopting healthy lifestyle habits, including a balanced diet, regular exercise, and other proactive measures, you can strengthen your bones and support long-term bone health.

It's never too early or too late to start taking care of your bones. Whether you're young or old, incorporating bone-friendly foods, engaging in weight-bearing exercises, and making positive lifestyle choices can make a significant difference in your bone health.

Think of your bones as the foundation of your body. By investing in their health now, you're laying the groundwork for a strong and resilient future. Take the time to prioritize bone health today, and your body will thank you for it tomorrow.

Don't wait until problems arise to start taking care of your bones. Empower yourself with knowledge, make informed choices, and seek support from healthcare professionals or fitness experts if needed. Your efforts toward maintaining strong and healthy bones will pay off in the long run, allowing you to live a vibrant and active life.

So, let's commit to prioritizing bone health together. With dedication, consistency, and a positive mindset, we can all take proactive steps toward building and maintaining strong bones for a lifetime of health and vitality.

Here's to strong bones and a brighter future ahead!

Warm regards, [Arielle Curbert]

C. Final thoughts and encouragement to explore the recipes in the cookbook

Dear Readers,

As you journey through the pages of this cookbook, I hope you feel inspired to embark on a delicious and nutritious adventure toward better bone health. Each recipe has been carefully crafted to provide you with the essential nutrients needed to support strong and resilient bones.

Remember, your health is your greatest asset, and prioritizing bone health is a vital step toward overall well-being. By incorporating these nutrient-rich and flavorful recipes into your daily meals, you're not only nourishing your body but also investing in your future health.

Whether you're enjoying a calcium-rich spinach and feta stuffed chicken breast, savoring the flavors of a protein-packed lentil and vegetable curry, or indulging in a refreshing kale and pineapple smoothie, each dish offers a delightful combination of taste and nutrition.

I encourage you to explore the recipes in this cookbook with enthusiasm and curiosity. Get creative in the kitchen, experiment with new ingredients, and discover the joy of cooking meals that support your bone health while tantalizing your taste buds.

Let this cookbook serve as a guide on your journey toward stronger bones and better health. Embrace the power of nutritious eating, stay active, and make self-care a priority in your daily life. Your body will thank you for it, and you'll enjoy the benefits of improved energy, vitality, and resilience.

So, dive into these recipes with enthusiasm and an open heart. Whether you're cooking for yourself, your family, or your friends, remember that each meal is an opportunity to nourish your body and nurture your well-being.

Here's to good health, happy cooking, and strong bones for life!

Warm regards,
[Arielle Curbert]

Bonus Section 1: Quick and Easy Bone-Boosting Snacks

A. Introduction to the importance of snacking for bone health

Snacking often gets a bad rap, especially when it comes to concerns about health and nutrition. However, when done right, snacking can be an essential component of a balanced diet, particularly when it comes to supporting bone health. Bones play a crucial role in our overall well-being, providing structure, protection, and support for our bodies. Therefore, it's vital to ensure they receive the nutrients they need to stay strong and healthy. In this article, we'll explore the importance of snacking for bone health and discover some nutritious snack options to support optimal bone strength.

1. **Nutrient Requirements for Bone Health:** Bones are primarily made up of calcium, along with other essential minerals like phosphorus and magnesium. Calcium, in particular, is vital for maintaining bone density and strength. Without an adequate intake of calcium, bones can become weak and prone to fractures and diseases like osteoporosis. Additionally, vitamin D plays a crucial role in calcium absorption, making it another essential nutrient for bone health. Snacking provides an excellent opportunity to incorporate these vital nutrients into your diet, helping to support strong and healthy bones.

2. **Balancing Snacks for Bone Health:** When choosing snacks to support bone health, it's essential to focus on options that are rich in calcium, vitamin D, and other bone-supporting nutrients. Opting for whole, nutrient-dense foods is key, as they provide a more significant nutritional punch compared to processed snacks high in sugar and unhealthy fats. Incorporating a mix of protein, healthy fats, and carbohydrates into your snacks can also help keep you feeling satisfied and energized throughout the day.

3. **Snack Ideas for Bone Health:** Here are some nutritious snack ideas to support bone health:
    a. **Greek Yogurt with Berries:** Greek yogurt is an excellent source of calcium and protein, while berries provide antioxidants and vitamin C, which is essential for collagen production. Mix them for a tasty and nutritious snack.
    b. **Almond Butter and Banana on Whole Grain Crackers:** Almond butter is rich in calcium, magnesium, and vitamin E, while bananas

provide potassium and vitamin B6. Spread almond butter on whole-grain crackers and top with banana slices for a satisfying snack.
   c. **Vegetable Sticks with Hummus:** Crunchy vegetables like carrots, celery, and bell peppers are packed with vitamins and minerals, including calcium and vitamin K, which are important for bone health. Pair them with hummus for a delicious and nutritious snack.
   d. **Cheese and Whole Grain Crackers:** Cheese is an excellent source of calcium and protein, making it a great choice for supporting bone health. Pair it with whole-grain crackers for a satisfying and convenient snack.
   e. **Trail Mix with Nuts and Seeds:** Nuts and seeds are rich in calcium, magnesium, and other essential nutrients for bone health. Mix them with dried fruit for a portable and nutritious snack option.
4. **Conclusion:** Snacking can be an excellent way to support bone health by providing essential nutrients like calcium, vitamin D, and magnesium. By choosing nutrient-dense snacks that incorporate a variety of food groups, you can help ensure that your bones stay strong and healthy. Incorporate some of the snack ideas mentioned above into your daily routine to promote optimal bone health and overall well-being. Remember to enjoy snacks in moderation and pay attention to portion sizes to maintain a balanced diet.

B. Recipes for convenient and nutritious snacks

1. **Greek Yogurt with Honey and Almonds:**
   - Ingredients:
     - 1 cup Greek yogurt
     - 1 tablespoon honey
     - 2 tablespoons sliced almonds
   - Preparation:
     - Spoon Greek yogurt into a bowl.
     - Drizzle honey over the yogurt.
     - Sprinkle sliced almonds on top.
   - Nutritional Information: Calories: 220, Protein: 20g, Fat: 9g, Carbohydrates: 18g
   - Cooking Time: 5 minutes

2. **Apple Slices with Peanut Butter:**
   - Ingredients:
     - 1 medium apple, sliced
     - 2 tablespoons peanut butter
   - Preparation:
     - Slice the apple into thin wedges.
     - Spread peanut butter on each apple slice.
   - Nutritional Information: Calories: 220, Protein: 6g, Fat: 14g, Carbohydrates: 22g
   - Cooking Time: 3 minutes

3. **Trail Mix with Dried Fruit and Pumpkin Seeds:**
   - Ingredients:
     - 1/2 cup dried cranberries
     - 1/2 cup dried apricots, chopped
     - 1/2 cup pumpkin seeds
     - 1/2 cup almonds
     - 1/2 cup cashews
   - Preparation:
     - Mix all ingredients in a bowl.
     - Divide into individual snack-sized portions.
   - Nutritional Information: Calories: 280, Protein: 8g, Fat: 16g, Carbohydrates: 30g
   - Cooking Time: 0 minutes

4. **Veggie Sticks with Hummus:**
   - Ingredients:
     - Carrot sticks, cucumber slices, and bell pepper strips.
     - 1/4 cup hummus
   - Preparation:
     - Wash and cut vegetables into sticks or slices.
     - Serve with a side of hummus for dipping.
   - Nutritional Information: Calories: 150, Protein: 5g, Fat: 8g, Carbohydrates: 15g

- Preparation Time: 5 minutes

5. Cottage Cheese with Berries:
- Ingredients:
  - 1/2 cup low-fat cottage cheese
  - 1/2 cup mixed berries (strawberries, blueberries, raspberries)
- Preparation:
  - Spoon cottage cheese into a bowl.
  - Top with mixed berries.
- Nutritional Information: Calories: 120, Protein: 12g, Fat: 2g, Carbohydrates: 15g
- Preparation Time: 2 minutes

6. Whole Grain Crackers with Tuna Salad:
- Ingredients:
  - Whole grain crackers
  - 1 can tuna, drained
  - 1 tablespoon mayonnaise
  - 1 tablespoon diced celery
  - Salt and pepper to taste
- Preparation:
  - In a bowl, mix tuna, mayonnaise, diced celery, salt, and pepper.
  - Spread tuna salad onto whole grain crackers.
- Nutritional Information: Calories: 180, Protein: 15g, Fat: 8g, Carbohydrates: 10g
- Preparation Time: 5 minutes

Bonus Section 2: Bone-Building Smoothie Bowls

A. Introduction to the benefits of smoothie bowls for bone health

Smoothie bowls have gained popularity in recent years as a delicious and nutritious breakfast or snack option. Beyond their vibrant colors and refreshing flavors, smoothie bowls offer a plethora of benefits for bone health. In this section, we'll explore why smoothie bowls are an excellent choice for supporting strong and healthy bones.

Our bones require a variety of nutrients to stay strong and resilient throughout life. Smoothie bowls provide an easy and convenient way to pack a wide range of bone-friendly nutrients into one delicious meal. From calcium-rich dairy products to vitamin D-packed fruits and leafy greens, smoothie bowl ingredients can be tailored to provide the essential nutrients needed for optimal bone health.

Furthermore, smoothie bowls offer versatility, allowing you to customize your blend based on your taste preferences and dietary needs. Whether you prefer a creamy base of yogurt or milk or a plant-based alternative like almond or coconut milk, smoothie bowls can be adapted to suit your individual preferences.

In addition to providing essential nutrients, smoothie bowls can also support hydration, which is important for overall bone health. Many fruits and vegetables used in smoothie bowls have high water content, helping to keep you hydrated throughout the day.

Moreover, smoothie bowls are easy to digest, making them an ideal option for individuals with digestive issues or those who may have difficulty absorbing nutrients from solid foods. The blending process breaks down fruits, vegetables, and other ingredients into a more easily digestible form, allowing your body to absorb nutrients more efficiently.

B. Recipes for vibrant and nutrient-packed smoothie bowl creations

1. **Acai Berry Smoothie Bowl with Granola and Chia Seeds:**
   - Ingredients:
     - 1 packet of frozen acai puree
     - 1/2 cup mixed berries (strawberries, blueberries, raspberries)
     - 1/2 banana
     - 1/4 cup almond milk

- Toppings: Granola, chia seeds, sliced strawberries
- Preparation:
    - Blend acai puree, mixed berries, banana, and almond milk until smooth.
    - Pour into a bowl and top with granola, chia seeds, and sliced strawberries.
- Nutritional Information: Calories: 300, Protein: 7g, Fat: 10g, Carbohydrates: 50g
- Preparation Time: 5 minutes

2. **Mango Tango Smoothie Bowl with Spinach and Coconut Flakes:**
   - Ingredients:
     - 1 cup frozen mango chunks
     - 1 handful spinach
     - 1/2 cup coconut water
     - Toppings: Sliced mango, coconut flakes, sliced almonds
   - Preparation:
     - Blend mango chunks, spinach, and coconut water until smooth.
     - Pour into a bowl and top with sliced mango, coconut flakes, and sliced almonds.
   - Nutritional Information: Calories: 250, Protein: 5g, Fat: 8g, Carbohydrates: 40g
   - Preparation Time: 5 minutes

3. **Blueberry Blast Smoothie Bowl with Greek Yogurt and Hemp Hearts:**
   - Ingredients:
     - 1/2 cup frozen blueberries
     - 1/2 cup Greek yogurt
     - 1 tablespoon honey
     - Toppings: Fresh blueberries, hemp hearts, sliced banana
   - Preparation:
     - Blend frozen blueberries, Greek yogurt, and honey until smooth.
     - Pour into a bowl and top with fresh blueberries, hemp hearts, and sliced banana.

- Nutritional Information: Calories: 280, Protein: 20g, Fat: 8g, Carbohydrates: 35g
- Preparation Time: 5 minutes

4. **Green Goddess Smoothie Bowl with Kale and Avocado:**
    - Ingredients:
        - 1 cup kale leaves, stems removed
        - 1/2 ripe avocado
        - 1/2 cup pineapple chunks
        - 1/2 cup coconut water
        - Toppings: sliced kiwi, shredded coconut, and pumpkin seeds
    - Preparation:
        - Blend kale leaves, avocado, pineapple chunks, and coconut water until smooth.
        - Pour into a bowl and top with sliced kiwi, shredded coconut, and pumpkin seeds.
    - Nutritional Information: Calories: 270, Protein: 6g, Fat: 15g, Carbohydrates: 30g
    - Preparation Time: 5 minutes

5. **Peanut Butter Power Smoothie Bowl with Banana and Cacao Nibs:**
    - Ingredients:
        - 2 tablespoons peanut butter
        - 1 frozen banana
        - 1/2 cup almond milk
        - 1 tablespoon cacao nibs
        - Toppings: Sliced banana, cacao nibs, granola
    - Preparation:
        - Blend peanut butter, frozen banana, almond milk, and cacao nibs until smooth.
        - Pour into a bowl and top with sliced banana, cacao nibs, and granola.
    - Nutritional Information: Calories: 320, Protein: 8g, Fat: 18g, Carbohydrates: 35g
    - Preparation Time: 5 minutes

Bonus Section 3: Family-Friendly Bone-Boosting Recipes

A. Introduction to the importance of involving the whole family in bone-healthy eating habits

Ensuring strong and healthy bones is not just an individual concern; it's a family affair. In this section, we'll explore the significance of involving the entire family in cultivating bone-healthy eating habits and lifestyle choices.

Our bones are the foundation of our bodies, providing structure, support, and protection. Building and maintaining strong bones is essential for overall health and well-being, particularly as we age. By instilling bone-healthy habits from an early age and fostering a supportive environment within the family, we can empower everyone to prioritize bone health and make informed dietary choices. Involving the whole family in bone-healthy eating habits fosters a sense of unity and shared responsibility. It allows family members to learn from each other, support one another, and collectively work towards a common goal of optimal bone health. By making bone-healthy eating a family priority, we can create a positive and supportive environment that encourages everyone to make nutritious food choices.

Furthermore, incorporating bone-healthy foods into family meals and snacks ensures that everyone receives the essential nutrients needed for strong and resilient bones. From calcium-rich dairy products to vitamin D-packed fish and leafy greens, there are plenty of delicious and nutritious options to suit every taste and preference.

By involving the whole family in meal planning, grocery shopping, and cooking, we can teach valuable life skills and instill a lifelong appreciation for healthy eating. Together, we can create a culture of wellness within the family that extends beyond the dinner table and into every aspect of daily life.

B. Recipes that appeal to both adults and children alike

1. **Turkey and Veggie Meatballs with Whole Wheat Pasta:**
    - Ingredients:
        - 1 pound ground turkey
        - 1/2 cup grated zucchini
        - 1/2 cup grated carrot

- 1/4 cup breadcrumbs
- 1 egg
- 1 teaspoon Italian seasoning
- Salt and pepper to taste
- 8 ounces whole wheat pasta
- 2 cups marinara sauce
- Preparation:
    - Preheat oven to 375°F (190°C).
    - In a large bowl, combine ground turkey, grated zucchini, grated carrot, breadcrumbs, egg, Italian seasoning, salt, and pepper. Mix until well combined.
    - Shape mixture into meatballs and place on a baking sheet lined with parchment paper.
    - Bake for 20 to 25 minutes, or until thoroughly cooked.
    - Meanwhile, cook the whole wheat pasta according to the package directions.
    - Serve meatballs over cooked pasta with marinara sauce.
- Nutritional Information: Calories: 350, Protein: 25g, Fat: 8g, Carbohydrates: 45g
- Cooking Time: 30 minutes

2. **Cheesy Cauliflower Mac and Cheese:**
    - Ingredients:
        - 1 head cauliflower, cut into florets
        - 8 ounces whole wheat elbow macaroni
        - 1 cup shredded cheddar cheese
        - 1/4 cup grated Parmesan cheese
        - 1/2 cup milk
        - 2 tablespoons butter
        - Salt and pepper to taste
    - Preparation:
        - Preheat oven to 375°F (190°C).
        - Steam cauliflower florets until tender, about 10 minutes.
        - Cook macaroni according to package instructions.

- In a large saucepan, melt the butter over medium heat. Mix in the milk, cheddar cheese, and Parmesan cheese until melted and smooth.
- Add steamed cauliflower to the cheese sauce and stir until well coated.
- Stir in cooked macaroni until evenly combined.
- Transfer mixture to a baking dish and bake for 20-25 minutes or until bubbly and golden on top.
  - Nutritional Information: Calories: 320, Protein: 15g, Fat: 12g, Carbohydrates: 40g
  - Cooking Time: 40 minutes

3. **Homemade Fruit and Yogurt Popsicles:**
   - Ingredients:
     - 2 cups plain Greek yogurt
     - 1 cup of mixed berries (strawberries, blueberries, raspberries)
     - 2 tablespoons honey
     - Popsicle molds
   - Preparation:
     - Blend Greek yogurt, mixed berries, and honey. Blend until completely smooth.
     - Pour mixture into popsicle molds.
     - Insert the popsicle sticks and freeze for at least 4 hours, or until firm.
     - To release popsicles, run molds under warm water for a few seconds.
   - Nutritional Information: Calories: 100, Protein: 8g, Fat: 2g, Carbohydrates: 15g
   - Cooking Time: 5 minutes + freezing time

4. **Veggie Quesadillas with Guacamole:**
   - Ingredients:
     - 4 whole wheat tortillas
     - 1 cup shredded cheddar cheese
     - 1 cup mixed bell peppers, thinly sliced

- 1/2 cup black beans (drained and rinsed)
- 1/2 cup corn kernels
- 1 avocado, mashed
- 1 tablespoon lime juice
- Salt and pepper to taste
- Preparation:
    - In a bowl, combine mashed avocado, lime juice, salt, and pepper to make guacamole.
    - Place a tortilla in a skillet over medium heat. Cover half of the tortilla with shredded cheese, bell peppers, black beans, and corn. Fold the remaining half of the tortilla over the filling.
    - Cook for 2-3 minutes per side, or until the tortilla is crisp and the cheese has melted.
    - Repeat with the remaining tortillas and filling ingredients.
    - Slice quesadillas into wedges and serve with guacamole.
- Nutritional Information: Calories: 280, Protein: 10g, Fat: 12g, Carbohydrates: 35g
- Cooking Time: 15 minutes

5. Baked Chicken Tenders with Sweet Potato Fries:
- Ingredients:
    - 1 pound chicken breast tenders
    - 1 cup whole wheat breadcrumbs
    - 1/4 cup grated Parmesan cheese
    - 1 teaspoon garlic powder
    - 1/2 teaspoon paprika
    - 2 eggs, beaten
    - 2 sweet potatoes, cut into fries
    - 1 tablespoon olive oil
    - Salt and pepper to taste
- Preparation:
    - Preheat oven to 400°F (200°C).
    - In a shallow dish, combine breadcrumbs, Parmesan cheese, garlic powder, and paprika.

- Dip chicken tenders in beaten eggs, then coat with breadcrumb mixture.
- Place the coated chicken tenders on a baking sheet lined with parchment paper.
- Toss sweet potato fries with olive oil, salt, and pepper, then spread them out on a separate baking sheet.
- Bake chicken tenders and sweet potato fries for 20-25 minutes or until golden and crispy.
- Serve with your favorite dipping sauce.
- Nutritional Information: Calories: 320, Protein: 25g, Fat: 10g, Carbohydrates: 30g
- Cooking Time: 25 minutes

6. **Veggie-packed Pizza with Whole Wheat Crust:**
    - Ingredients:
        - 1 whole wheat pizza crust
        - 1/2 cup marinara sauce
        - 1 cup shredded mozzarella cheese
        - Assorted vegetables (bell peppers, mushrooms, onions, spinach, etc.)
        - Optional toppings: Cooked chicken, turkey pepperoni, olives
    - Preparation:
        - Preheat oven to 425°F (220°C).
        - Spread the marinara sauce evenly on the pizza crust.
        - Sprinkle shredded mozzarella cheese over the sauce.
        - Arrange assorted vegetables and any optional toppings over the cheese.
        - Bake the pizza in the preheated oven for 12-15 minutes, or until the crust is golden and the cheese is melted.
        - Slice and serve hot.
    - Nutritional Information: Calories: 280, Protein: 15g, Fat: 10g, Carbohydrates: 35g
    - Cooking Time: 15 minutes

7. **Crunchy Veggie and Hummus Wraps:**
   - Ingredients:
     - Whole wheat wraps or tortillas
     - Hummus
     - Assorted crunchy vegetables (carrots, cucumbers, bell peppers, lettuce, etc.)
     - Optional additions: Sliced turkey or chicken, avocado slices
   - Preparation:
     - Spread a generous layer of hummus onto each wrap or tortilla.
     - Layer crunchy vegetables and any optional additions over the hummus.
     - Roll up the wraps tightly and slice them in half.
     - Serve as is or with a side of fruit or salad.
   - Nutritional Information: Calories: 250, Protein: 8g, Fat: 10g, Carbohydrates: 30g
   - Preparation Time: 10 minutes

8. **Fruit and Nut Butter Sandwiches:**
   - Ingredients:
     - Whole grain bread
     - Nut butter (peanut butter, almond butter, etc.)
     - Sliced fruit (banana, apple, berries, etc.)
     - Optional additions: Honey, cinnamon, chia seeds
   - Preparation:
     - Spread nut butter on one slice of bread.
     - Arrange sliced fruit over the nut butter.
     - Drizzle with honey and sprinkle with cinnamon or chia seeds if desired.
     - Top with the second slice of bread and gently press to seal.
   - Nutritional Information: Calories: 300, Protein: 10g, Fat: 12g, Carbohydrates: 40g
   - Preparation Time: 5 minutes

9. Banana and Oatmeal Breakfast Muffins:
- Ingredients:
  - 2 ripe bananas, mashed
  - 2 cups rolled oats
  - 1/4 cup honey or maple syrup
  - 1/4 cup of milk (or almond milk for dairy-free option)
  - 1 teaspoon vanilla extract
  - 1 teaspoon baking powder
  - 1/2 teaspoon cinnamon
  - Pinch of salt
  - Optional add-ins: chopped nuts, chocolate chips, dried fruit
- Preparation:
  - Preheat the oven to 350°F (175°C). Line a muffin tin with paper liners.
  - In a large bowl, mix mashed bananas, rolled oats, honey or maple syrup, milk, vanilla extract, baking powder, cinnamon, and salt until well combined.
  - If desired, stir in optional add-ins such as chopped nuts, chocolate chips, or dried fruit.
  - Divide the batter evenly into the muffin cups.
  - Bake for 20-25 minutes, until golden brown and a toothpick inserted in the center comes out clean.
  - Allow muffins to cool in their tins for 5 minutes before transferring to a wire rack to finish cooling.
- Nutritional Information: Calories: 150, Protein: 4g, Fat: 2g, Carbohydrates: 30g
- Cooking Time: 25 minutes

10. Veggie and Cheese Quesadilla Dippers:
- Ingredients:
  - Whole wheat tortillas
  - 1 cup of shredded cheese.
  - Assorted vegetable fillings (bell peppers, onions, tomatoes, spinach)
  - Salsa or guacamole for dipping
- Preparation:
  - Preheat a nonstick skillet to medium heat.
  - Place a tortilla in the skillet and sprinkle shredded cheese evenly over one-half of the tortilla.

- Add desired vegetable fillings on top of the cheese.
- Fold the other half of the tortilla over the fillings to form a half-moon shape.
- Cook for 2-3 minutes per side, or until the tortilla is crisp and the cheese has melted. 3
- Slice quesadilla into wedges and serve with salsa or guacamole for dipping.
- Nutritional Information: Calories: 200, Protein: 8g, Fat: 10g, Carbohydrates: 20g
- Cooking Time: 10 minutes

Bonus Section 4: Plant-Based Powerhouses for Strong Bones

A. Introduction to plant-based eating for bone health

Plant-based eating has gained widespread recognition for its numerous health benefits, including its potential to support bone health. In this section, we'll explore the principles of plant-based eating and how it can contribute to strong and resilient bones.

Plant-based eating emphasizes the consumption of whole, minimally processed foods derived from plants, such as fruits, vegetables, whole grains, legumes, nuts, and seeds. This dietary approach is rich in essential nutrients, including calcium, magnesium, potassium, vitamin K, and phytonutrients, which are all vital for maintaining optimal bone health.

One of the key advantages of plant-based eating for bone health is its abundance of alkaline-forming foods. While animal-based foods tend to be acid-forming, leading to increased acidity in the body, many plant-based foods have an alkalizing effect, helping to balance pH levels and reduce calcium loss from the bones.

Additionally, plant-based diets are typically lower in dietary acid load, which has been associated with reduced risk of osteoporosis and fractures. By emphasizing plant foods and minimizing the consumption of animal products and processed foods, individuals can create a dietary environment that is conducive to bone health.

Furthermore, plant-based eating offers a wide variety of nutrient-dense foods that provide a rich array of vitamins, minerals, antioxidants, and phytonutrients that support overall health and well-being. From leafy greens packed with calcium and vitamin K to nuts and seeds rich in magnesium and phosphorus, plant-based foods offer a holistic approach to nourishing the body and supporting bone health.

B. Recipes showcasing the abundance of bone-boosting plant foods

1. **Quinoa and Black Bean Stuffed Bell Peppers:**
   - Ingredients:
     - 4 bell peppers, halved and seeds removed
     - 1 cup cooked quinoa
     - 1 cup black beans, cooked or canned, drained and rinsed
     - 1/2 cup corn kernels

- 1/2 cup diced tomatoes
- 1/2 cup diced onion
- 1 teaspoon cumin
- 1 teaspoon chili powder
- Salt and pepper to taste
- Optional toppings include avocado slices, chopped cilantro, and lime wedges.
- Preparation:
    - Preheat oven to 375°F (190°C).
    - In a large mixing bowl, combine cooked quinoa, black beans, corn kernels, diced tomatoes, onion, cumin, chili powder, salt, and pepper.
    - Stuff each bell pepper half with the quinoa and black bean mixture.
    - Place stuffed bell peppers in a baking dish and cover with aluminum foil.
    - Bake for 25-30 minutes or until bell peppers are tender.
    - Serve hot, with optional toppings as desired.
- Nutritional Information: Calories: 200, Protein: 8g, Fat: 2g, Carbohydrates: 40g
- Cooking Time: 35 minutes

2. **Lentil and Sweet Potato Shepherd's Pie:**
    - Ingredients:
        - 2 cups cooked lentils
        - 2 cups mashed sweet potatoes
        - 1 onion, diced
        - 2 carrots, diced
        - 2 celery stalks, diced
        - 2 garlic cloves, minced
        - 1 cup vegetable broth
        - 1 tablespoon tomato paste
        - 1 teaspoon dried thyme
        - Salt and pepper to taste
    - Preparation:

- Preheat oven to 375°F (190°C).
- In a skillet, sauté diced onion, carrots, celery, and garlic until softened.
- Add cooked lentils, vegetable broth, tomato paste, dried thyme, salt, and pepper to the skillet. Cook until heated through.
- Transfer the lentil mixture to a baking dish and spread mashed sweet potatoes evenly over the top.
- Bake for 25-30 minutes or until the sweet potatoes are lightly golden.
- Serve hot and enjoy!
- Nutritional Information: Calories: 250, Protein: 10g, Fat: 1g, Carbohydrates: 50g
- Cooking Time: 45 minutes

3. **Vegan Creamy Broccoli Soup with Cashew Cream:**
    - Ingredients:
        - 4 cups chopped broccoli florets
        - 1 onion, diced
        - 2 garlic cloves, minced
        - 4 cups vegetable broth
        - 1/2 cup of raw cashews, soaked in water for 4 hours or overnight
        - 1 tablespoon nutritional yeast
        - Salt and pepper to taste
    - Preparation:
        - In a large pot, cook the diced onion and garlic until softened.
        - Add chopped broccoli florets and vegetable broth to the pot. Bring to a boil, then reduce heat and simmer until broccoli is tender.
        - Meanwhile, drain soaked cashews and place them in a blender with enough water to cover. Blend until smooth and creamy.
        - Stir cashew cream and nutritional yeast into the soup. Add salt and pepper to taste.
        - Serve hot and garnish with a sprinkle of nutritional yeast, if desired.

- Nutritional Information: Calories: 180, Protein: 8g, Fat: 10g, Carbohydrates: 20g
- Cooking Time: 30 minutes

4. **Vegan Spinach and Chickpea Curry:**
    - Ingredients:
        - 2 tablespoons olive oil
        - 1 onion, diced
        - 3 cloves garlic, minced
        - 1 tablespoon ginger, minced
        - 2 teaspoons curry powder
        - 1 teaspoon ground cumin
        - 1 teaspoon ground coriander
        - 1/2 teaspoon turmeric
        - 1/4 teaspoon cayenne pepper (optional)
        - 1 can (14 oz) diced tomatoes
        - 1 can (14 oz) coconut milk
        - 1 can (14 oz) chickpeas, drained and rinsed
        - 4 cups fresh spinach
        - Salt and pepper to taste
        - Cooked brown rice, for serving
    - Preparation:
        - In a large skillet, heat the olive oil over medium heat. Cook for about 5 minutes, or until the diced onion has softened.
        - Add minced garlic and ginger, and cook for another minute until fragrant.
        - Stir in curry powder, cumin, coriander, turmeric, and cayenne pepper (if using), and cook for 1-2 minutes until spices are toasted.
        - Add diced tomatoes and coconut milk to the skillet, and bring to a simmer.
        - Stir in chickpeas and fresh spinach, and cook until spinach wilts and chickpeas are heated through.
        - Season with salt and pepper to taste.
        - Serve the curry over cooked brown rice and enjoy!

- Nutritional Information: Calories: 350, Protein: 10g, Fat: 20g, Carbohydrates: 35g
- Cooking Time: 30 minutes

5. **Roasted Brussels Sprouts and Butternut Squash Salad:**
    - Ingredients:
        - 2 cups Brussels sprouts, halved
        - 2 cups butternut squash, diced
        - 2 tablespoons olive oil
        - 1 tablespoon balsamic vinegar
        - 1 teaspoon maple syrup
        - Salt and pepper to taste
        - 1/4 cup dried cranberries
        - 1/4 cup chopped walnuts
        - 2 cups mixed greens
        - Lemon vinaigrette dressing (optional)
    - Preparation:
        - Preheat oven to 400°F (200°C).
        - Toss Brussels sprouts and butternut squash with olive oil, balsamic vinegar, maple syrup, salt, and pepper.
        - Spread vegetables in a single layer on a baking sheet lined with parchment paper.
        - Roast for 20-25 minutes or until vegetables are tender and caramelized.
        - In a large mixing bowl, toss roasted Brussels sprouts and butternut squash with dried cranberries, chopped walnuts, and mixed greens.
        - Drizzle with lemon vinaigrette dressing, if desired, and toss to coat.
        - Serve warm or at room temperature.
    - Nutritional Information: Calories: 250, Protein: 5g, Fat: 15g, Carbohydrates: 25g
    - Cooking Time: 30 minutes

Bonus Section 5: Bone-Building Brunch Ideas

A. Introduction to the versatility of brunch options that support bone health

Brunch, often celebrated as a leisurely and indulgent meal, offers a wonderful opportunity to incorporate bone-boosting ingredients into your diet while enjoying delicious and satisfying dishes. In this section, we'll explore the versatility of brunch options that not only tantalize the taste buds but also provide essential nutrients to support optimal bone health.

Brunch encompasses a wide range of dishes, from savory to sweet, and allows for creativity in combining flavors and ingredients. By selecting wholesome and nutrient-dense foods, you can create brunch options that are not only delicious but also nourishing for your bones.

One of the key components of a bone-healthy brunch is the incorporation of foods rich in calcium, vitamin D, magnesium, and other essential nutrients. From leafy greens and fortified plant-based milk to nuts, seeds, and whole grains, countless ingredients can be incorporated into brunch recipes to support bone health.

Additionally, brunch offers the opportunity to include a variety of plant-based proteins such as beans, lentils, tofu, and tempeh, which are not only rich in protein but also contain important minerals like calcium and magnesium. By incorporating these plant-based proteins into your brunch options, you can enhance the nutrient density of your meal while supporting bone health.

B. Recipes for hearty and nutritious brunch dishes perfect for weekend gatherings

1. **Spinach and Mushroom Frittata:**
   - Ingredients:
     - 8 eggs
     - 1 cup chopped spinach
     - 1 cup sliced mushrooms
     - 1/2 cup diced onion
     - 1/4 cup shredded cheese (optional)
     - 2 tablespoons olive oil
     - Salt and pepper to taste
   - Preparation:

- Preheat the oven to 350°F (175°C).
- In a mixing bowl, combine the eggs, salt, and pepper until thoroughly combined.
- Heat the olive oil in an oven-safe skillet over medium heat. Sauté diced onion and sliced mushrooms until softened.
- Cook the chopped spinach in the skillet until wilted.
- Pour the whisked eggs over the vegetables in the skillet, ensuring an even distribution.
- If using, sprinkle the top with shredded cheese.
- Place the skillet in the preheated oven for 15-20 minutes, or until the frittata is set and slightly golden on top.
- Remove from the oven, cut into wedges, and serve hot.
- Nutritional Information: Calories: 200, Protein: 15g, Fat: 12g, Carbohydrates: 5g
- Cooking Time: 25 minutes

2. **Whole Wheat Banana Pancakes with Berries and Greek Yogurt:**
   - Ingredients:
     - 1 cup whole wheat flour
     - 1 ripe banana, mashed
     - 1 cup milk (or plant-based milk)
     - 1 egg
     - 1 tablespoon honey or maple syrup
     - 1 teaspoon baking powder
     - 1/2 teaspoon cinnamon
     - Pinch of salt
     - Mixed berries and Greek yogurt, for topping
   - Preparation:
     - In a mixing bowl, combine whole wheat flour, mashed banana, milk, egg, honey or maple syrup, baking powder, cinnamon, and salt. Mix until smooth.
     - Heat a non-stick skillet or griddle over medium heat and lightly grease with oil or cooking spray.
     - Pour approximately 1/4 cup batter into the skillet for each pancake.

- Cook for 2-3 minutes, or until bubbles appear on top of the pancake. Flip and cook for another 1-2 minutes, or until golden brown.
			- Repeat with the remaining batter.
			- Serve the pancakes topped with mixed berries and a dollop of Greek yogurt.
	- Nutritional Information: Calories: 250, Protein: 10g, Fat: 5g, Carbohydrates: 40g
	- Cooking Time: 20 minutes

3. **Smashed Avocado Toast with Poached Eggs and Tomato Salsa:**
	- Ingredients:
		- 4 slices whole wheat bread, toasted
		- 2 ripe avocados
		- 4 eggs, poached
		- 1 cup diced tomatoes
		- 1/4 cup diced red onion
		- 1/4 cup chopped cilantro
		- 1 tablespoon lime juice
		- Salt and pepper to taste
	- Preparation:
		- Smash the ripe avocados in a bowl with a fork until smooth. Add salt and pepper to taste.
		- In another bowl, combine diced tomatoes, diced red onion, chopped cilantro, lime juice, salt, and pepper to make the tomato salsa.
		- Spread mashed avocado evenly onto each slice of toasted whole wheat bread.
		- Top each avocado toast with a poached egg.
		- Spoon tomato salsa over the poached eggs.
		- Serve immediately and enjoy!
	- Nutritional Information: Calories: 300, Protein: 15g, Fat: 15g, Carbohydrates: 25g
	- Cooking Time: 15 minutes

4. Sweet Potato and Black Bean Breakfast Burritos:

- Ingredients:
    - 4 large whole wheat tortillas
    - 2 cups cooked sweet potatoes, diced
    - 1 can (15 oz) of black beans, drained and rinsed
    - 1 bell pepper, diced
    - 1/2 cup diced onion
    - 1 teaspoon ground cumin
    - 1/2 teaspoon chili powder
    - Salt and pepper to taste
    - 1/2 cup shredded cheese (optional)
    - Salsa and avocado slices for serving
- Preparation:
    - In a skillet, sauté diced bell pepper and onion until softened.
    - Add cooked sweet potatoes, black beans, ground cumin, chili powder, salt, and pepper to the skillet. Cook until heated through.
    - Warm the whole wheat tortillas in a separate skillet or microwave.
    - Divide the sweet potato-black bean mixture evenly among the tortillas.
    - Sprinkle shredded cheese over the filling, if using.
    - Fold the sides of each tortilla over the filling, then roll tightly to make a burrito.
    - Serve the breakfast burritos with a side of salsa and avocado slices.
- Nutritional Information: Calories: 350, Protein: 12g, Fat: 8g, Carbohydrates: 60g
- Cooking Time: 20 minutes

5. Vegan Breakfast Hash with Tofu and Vegetables:

- Ingredients:
    - 1 firm tofu block (14 oz), drained and crumbled
    - 2 tablespoons olive oil
    - 2 cups diced potatoes
    - 1 bell pepper, diced
    - 1/2 cup diced onion
    - 2 cloves garlic, minced
    - 1 teaspoon smoked paprika
    - 1/2 teaspoon turmeric
    - Salt and pepper to taste
    - Fresh parsley for garnish
- Preparation:
    - In a medium-sized skillet, heat the olive oil. Add the diced potatoes and cook until golden and crispy.
    - Add diced bell pepper, onion, and minced garlic to the skillet. Cook until vegetables are tender.
    - Stir in crumbled tofu, smoked paprika, turmeric, salt, and pepper. Cook until tofu is heated through.
    - Serve the breakfast hash hot, garnished with fresh parsley.
- Nutritional Information: Calories: 300, Protein: 15g, Fat: 12g, Carbohydrates: 30g
- Cooking Time: 25 minutes

Yoga Exercises For Stronger And Healthy Bones

1. **Mountain Pose (Tadasana):**
    - Stand tall with your feet hip-width apart.
    - Keep your spine straight and shoulders relaxed.
    - Engage your leg muscles and lift your kneecaps.
    - Raise your arms overhead, palms facing each other.
    - Hold the pose for several breaths, focusing on lengthening your spine and maintaining balance.

2. **Tree Pose (Vrksasana):**
    - Start in Mountain Pose.
    - Transfer your weight to your left foot and lift your right foot off the ground.
    - Place the sole of your right foot against the inside of your left thigh or calf, avoiding the knee.
    - Place your hands in a prayer position at your chest or extend them overhead.
    - Keep your gaze steady and find a focal point to help with balance.
    - Hold the pose for a few breaths before switching sides.

3. **Triangle Pose (Trikonasana):**
    - Begin in a wide-legged stance with your feet approximately 3-4 feet apart.
    - Turn your right foot out 90 degrees while keeping your left foot slightly in.
    - Extend your arms out to the sides, shoulder height.
    - Reach your right hand towards your right ankle, shin, or a block placed on the outside of your right foot.
    - Extend your left arm towards the sky, keeping both arms in line with your shoulders.
    - Keep your torso open and facing to the side, with your chest lifted.
    - Hold the pose for a few breaths before switching sides.

4. **Bridge Pose (Setu Bandhasana):**
    - Lie on your back, knees bent, feet flat on the ground, hip-width apart.
    - Place your arms alongside your body, palms down.

- Press into your feet and lift your hips towards the ceiling, engaging your glutes and core.
- Roll your shoulders underneath you and clasp your hands together, or keep your arms flat on the ground.
- Keep your neck long and gaze towards your knees.
- Hold the pose for a few breaths before slowly lowering your hips back down.

5. **Chair Pose (Utkatasana):**
    - Begin in Mountain Pose.
    - Inhale as you raise your arms overhead, palms facing each other.
    - Exhale as you bend your knees and lower your hips as if sitting back in a chair.
    - Maintain a lifted chest and engaged core.
    - Hold the pose for several breaths, then straighten your legs to come back to standing.

Printed in Great Britain
by Amazon